CSS Refactoring
Architect Your Stylesheets for Success

Steve Lindstrom

Beijing · Boston · Farnham · Sebastopol · Tokyo

CSS Refactoring

by Steve Lindstrom

Printed in the United States of America.

Published by O'Reilly Media, Inc., 1005 Gravenstein Highway North, Sebastopol, CA 95472.

O'Reilly books may be purchased for educational, business, or sales promotional use. Online editions are also available for most titles (*http://oreilly.com/safari*). For more information, contact our corporate/institutional sales department: 800-998-9938 or *corporate@oreilly.com*.

Editor: Meg Foley	**Indexer:** Ellen Troutman-Zaig
Production Editor: Kristen Brown	**Interior Designer:** David Futato
Copyeditor: Rachel Head	**Cover Designer:** Karen Montgomery
Proofreader: Molly Ives Brower	**Illustrator:** Rebecca Demarest

November 2016:   First Edition

Revision History for the First Edition
2016-11-08:   First Release

See *http://oreilly.com/catalog/errata.csp?isbn=9781491906422* for release details.

978-1-491-90642-2

[LSI]

To my family, who have supported me through thick and thin; I wouldn't be where I am today without you.

Table of Contents

Preface

When I first started learning CSS, I found that getting to grips with the *syntax* (the set of rules and structures that comprise a programming language) was simple because there are rules that explain how the code should be written. However, I found it was much more difficult to learn how to keep my CSS organized and maintainable, and even more difficult to clean up the disorganized CSS I'd written without a clear vision. I wrote this book with the hope that I could help others by sharing everything I learned through trial and error; I wish this book had existed when I was just starting out.

Intended Audience

While I hope that anybody writing CSS will benefit from reading this book, it's aimed primarily at people who have cobbled together a working user interface but lack either the experience or the vision to understand how their code fits together in the bigger picture. The intended reader understands how to write CSS syntax, but might not necessarily grasp why some things work the way they do. They might also not know how to better architect their code into a piece of software that is easier to maintain, extend, and collaborate on.

Objectives of This Book

My goal in writing this book is to make some of the subtler aspects of CSS more approachable to readers that are just starting out. I also aim to shed some light on why CSS can be difficult to write and test and why spending time refactoring CSS is a worthwhile endeavor.

Topics we'll cover include:

- What refactoring is, why it's beneficial, and how it relates to software architecture
- Commonly misunderstood aspects of CSS including the cascade, selector specificity, and the box model
- How to write better CSS by making informed decisions and being consistent
- How to maintain well-written CSS with coding standards and pattern libraries
- How to test CSS
- How to organize CSS
- Strategies for refactoring CSS
- Ways to measure success when refactoring

Reading this book will provide the knowledge necessary to take immediate action to start working toward a better CSS codebase that should also be more maintainable when working with a team. While doing so, readers are encouraged to revisit chapters that apply to concepts they're currently making use of.

What's Not In This Book

This book focuses on explaining concepts that are not necessarily technical in nature. As such, there are a lot of topics that are not covered in this book. These include:

CSS properties
> Knowledge of available CSS properties is necessary for writing CSS, but they will not be covered in this book. While there may be recommendations for which properties to use from time to time, these properties are better learned by consulting a book like *CSS: The Definitive Guide* by Eric Meyer or *CSS Cookbook* by Christopher Schmitt (both from O'Reilly), or any number of reputable websites like the Mozilla Developer Network (*https://developer.mozilla.org*).

Structuring HTML
> HTML and CSS are used in tandem to build user interfaces, and one can influence the other. Strategies for decoupling CSS from HTML will be discussed, but the pros and cons of how to write and structure HTML will not.

Frontend performance
> Frontend performance is an important aspect of building any website, and it's an extremely interesting topic. Since this book is only about refactoring CSS, though, this topic will only be covered very briefly—it is far too broad a topic, since it encompasses a variety of other subjects. Steve Souders (*https://stevesoud ers.com*) has written some great books about performance, and Paul Irish (*http://www.paulirish.com*), Nicole Sullivan (*http://www.stubbornella.org*), and Stoyan

Stefanov (*http://www.phpied.com*) have done a lot of great work on the topic as well. Google also provides a number of guidelines and tools (*https://develop ers.google.com/speed/pagespeed*) that can be very beneficial to frontend performance.

CSS frameworks
CSS frameworks change frequently and impose their own rules on implementation, so they won't be covered in this book. However, after reading this book I hope that you will be able to look at the source code of any given framework and draw your own conclusions about its implementation.

Lesser-known or less popular browsers
There are a ton of web browsers out there, but I'll only be discussing the major players—Microsoft Edge (formerly Internet Explorer), Safari, Chrome, and Firefox, as well as their mobile counterparts—because they comprise the majority of the market share.

Nomenclature

Although the intended audience for this book has some knowledge about CSS, some nomenclature might not be familiar, so various terms will be defined throughout the book. At an even more basic level:

- *Selectors* are patterns that are used to choose an element or group of elements to style.
- A *declaration block* is a collection of rules that denote the properties and values that should be applied to an HTML element.
- A *property* indicates which style should be applied to the selected elements and is assigned a *value*.
- A *ruleset* is comprised of one or more selectors combined with a declaration block.

In Example P-1 the web browser is instructed to style all paragraphs such that they have blue text set at 16 px (pixels). p is the selector that tells the browser which elements to style. Everything from the left curly brace up to and including the right curly brace is the declaration block. The declaration block contains two declarations; the first assigns the value #1200FF to the color property and the second assigns the value 16px to the font-size property. The passage of code in its entirety is the ruleset. For your convenience, the anatomy of a ruleset is illustrated in Figure P-1.

Example P-1. A sample ruleset

```
p {
    color: #1200FF;
    font-size: 16px;
}
```

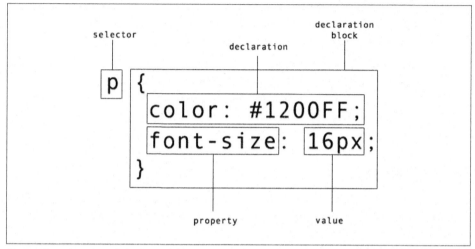

Figure P-1. Diagram of a CSS ruleset

What You'll Find on the Companion Website

The companion website to this book, *http://www.cssrefactoringbook.com*, contains:

- Examples from this book
- Occasional blog posts
- Links to great articles, presentations, and other resources
- Errata and corrections

This book is here to help you get your job done. In general, if example code is offered with this book, you may use it in your programs and documentation. You do not need to contact us for permission unless you're reproducing a significant portion of the code. For example, writing a program that uses several chunks of code from this book does not require permission. Selling or distributing a CD-ROM of examples from O'Reilly books does require permission. Answering a question by citing this book and quoting example code does not require permission. Incorporating a significant amount of example code from this book into your product's documentation does require permission.

We appreciate, but do not require, attribution. An attribution usually includes the title, author, publisher, and ISBN. For example: "*CSS Refactoring* by Steve Lindstrom (O'Reilly). Copyright 2017 Steve Lindstrom, 978-1-491-90642-2."

If you feel your use of code examples falls outside fair use or the permission given above, feel free to contact us at *permissions@oreilly.com*.

Conventions Used in This Book

The following typographical conventions are used in this book:

Italic
> Indicates new terms, URLs, email addresses, filenames, and file extensions.

`Constant width`
> Used for program listings, as well as within paragraphs to refer to program elements such as variable or function names, databases, data types, environment variables, statements, and keywords.

`Constant width bold`
> Shows commands or other text that should be typed literally by the user.

`Constant width italic`
> Shows text that should be replaced with user-supplied values or by values determined by context.

This element signifies a tip or suggestion.

This element signifies a general note.

This element indicates a warning or caution.

O'Reilly Safari

 *Safari* (formerly Safari Books Online) is membership-based training and reference platform for enterprise, government, educators, and individuals.

Members have access to thousands of books, training videos, Learning Paths, interactive tutorials, and curated playlists from over 250 publishers, including O'Reilly Media, Harvard Business Review, Prentice Hall Professional, Addison-Wesley Professional, Microsoft Press, Sams, Que, Peachpit Press, Adobe, Focal Press, Cisco Press, John Wiley & Sons, Syngress, Morgan Kaufmann, IBM Redbooks, Packt, Adobe Press, FT Press, Apress, Manning, New Riders, McGraw-Hill, Jones & Bartlett, and Course Technology, among others.

For more information, please visit *http://oreilly.com/safari*.

How to Contact Us

Please address comments and questions concerning this book to the publisher:

O'Reilly Media, Inc.
1005 Gravenstein Highway North
Sebastopol, CA 95472
800-998-9938 (in the United States or Canada)
707-829-0515 (international or local)
707-829-0104 (fax)

We have a web page for this book, where we list errata, examples, and any additional information. You can access this page at *http://bit.ly/css-refactoring*.

To comment or ask technical questions about this book, send email to *bookquestions@oreilly.com*.

For more information about our books, courses, conferences, and news, see our website at *http://www.oreilly.com*.

Find us on Facebook: *http://facebook.com/oreilly*

Follow us on Twitter: *http://twitter.com/oreillymedia*

Watch us on YouTube: *http://www.youtube.com/oreillymedia*

Acknowledgments

Writing this book was a truly humbling experience.

One night on a whim I sent a short proposal to O'Reilly Media in the form of a terse email that included some bullet points for ideas I had for this book. I panicked after the email was sent, and promptly stopped thinking about it because I didn't expect to hear back anyway.

When I did hear back from O'Reilly and it was good news I was even more afraid that I was in over my head, but Simon St. Laurent, Brian MacDonald, and Meg Foley were fantastic to work with. I owe a tremendous amount of gratitude to my editor Meg Foley in particular, because she was so understanding and encouraging despite the fact that I missed every single deadline that I had. I've said it before and I'll say it again—sorry Meg!

This book is full of techniques, strategies, and ideas that have come from lots of different places over the years. I can't claim ownership of the majority of the concepts in this book, so first and foremost I'd like to thank all of the people that have come before me and figured all of this stuff out. I think the web development community is one of the best to be a part of because there are so many smart people that are willing to share their ideas with everyone. I can only hope that I've done some good by compiling all of these ideas in one place.

Writing a book is much more difficult than I had ever imagined because it's time-consuming, lonely work, but fortunately I'm surrounded by great people all day at work. Whenever I felt like throwing in the towel writing this book, I would look to Andy Denmark's amazing work ethic for inspiration. Thor Denmark also helped me keep my head above water by showing me how to maintain a great attitude through both the good times and the bad. Nate Racklyeft and Josh Hudner read a very early version of this book and provided tremendous feedback that made it a thousand times better than it would have been otherwise. Finally, Erin Wallace provided valuable feedback as someone who deals with similar concepts of organization, process, and subtlety in the design world and was able to help me refine my writing to be easier to understand. All of these people keep me on my toes on a daily basis and push me to be better than I was the day before, and for that I'm eternally grateful.

I also owe a great deal of thanks to Christopher Schmitt for reviewing the contents of this book. When I found out that he was reviewing my work I knew that his name sounded familiar, and sure enough two of his books were sitting on my bookshelf. Your notes helped me immensely and your books were invaluable when I was first getting started. Thanks so much for taking the time out of your day to help a complete stranger. I'd love to repay the favor some day!

This acknowledgments section wouldn't be complete if I didn't also thank my family for making me the person I am today. My parents always encouraged me to read and I still try to read more than I watch TV. At an early age my dad gave me my first O'Reilly book (I think it was a book about C), and I attribute my career choice in large part to his encouragement and career. My mom and brother have also been major sources of inspiration and encouragement, and I can't possibly thank you enough.

Finally, I owe a lot of thanks to coffee. I love you, coffee <3.

CHAPTER 1

Refactoring and Architecture

This is the starting point of our CSS refactoring journey. In this chapter we'll learn what refactoring is and how it relates to software architecture. We'll also discuss the importance of refactoring and some of the reasons why your code might need it, and we'll also work through two refactoring examples to drive these concepts home.

What Is Refactoring?

Refactoring is the process of rewriting code in order to make it more simple and reusable without changing its behavior. It's a vital skill to have if you're writing code because you will have to do it at some point, whether you want to or not; you may have even already refactored code without realizing it! Since refactoring doesn't change the code's behavior it's understandable to wonder why it's even worth doing in the first place. However, before that question can be answered it's important to understand what software architecture is.

What Is Software Architecture?

Like a living creature, a software system is usually comprised of many smaller pieces that specialize in doing one particular thing. When combined, these smaller pieces work together to create the larger software system. *Software architecture* is the term used for describing how all of the pieces of a software project fit together.

Every piece of software, from a simple website to the control system in a spacecraft, has an architecture, whether it's intentional or not. However, the best architectures are usually planned out well before any coding takes place. Following are some of the most important characteristics of a good architecture.

Good Architectures Are Predictable

Being *predictable* means that accurate assumptions can be made about how the software works and is structured. Predictability is indicative of proper forward planning and will help save on development time because there will be no question as to:

- What a component's responsibilities are
- Where to find a particular piece of code
- Where to put a new piece of code

Because assumptions can be made accurately in a predictable architecture, developers that are unfamiliar with the code should be able to understand it more quickly.

Good Architectures Promote Code Reuse

Code reuse is the ability for code to be used in multiple places without being duplicated. Code reuse is beneficial because it speeds up development time, since you don't have to rewrite pieces of code that already exist. Similarly, the fewer pieces of code you have that solve a particular problem, the less time you will have to spend maintaining all of those implementations. For example, if you discover a bug in a piece of code that gets reused across a project, you know that bug will be present wherever that code is used. But by fixing it in one place, you'll fix it in all of the places that piece of code is used.

Good Architectures Are Extensible

Extensibility is a principle of good architecture because it allows for the system to have new functionality built upon it with ease. Most software isn't built from start to finish in one day, so it's very important that it can be built incrementally without requiring major structural changes. If your project frequently requires significant changes to its architecture it becomes much more difficult to release.

Good Architectures Are Maintainable

Much like extensibility, *maintainability* is very important to an architecture because it allows you to modify existing functionality with ease. Over time requirements may change, and you will be forced to modify your code. Having maintainable software means that you will be able to modify one piece of your code without necessarily having to drastically change all of the other pieces.

Software Architecture and Refactoring

In a nutshell, refactoring exists to help maintain and promote good software architecture. It is nothing more than a set of techniques that can be used to reorganize code into a more meaningful structure with the intention of making it more predictable, reusable, extensible, and maintainable. When your software's architecture displays the aforementioned characteristics it will be much more reliable for its intended users, and it will be much more enjoyable for you to work on too.

Shortcomings that Lead to Refactoring

Why isn't code just written correctly in the first place so there's no need to refactor it later? Despite our best efforts to design and write the highest-quality code possible, over time *something* will change that requires refactoring. Let's take a look at a few of the causes.

Changing Requirements

Over time software systems evolve as the result of changing requirements. When software is written to satisfy one set of requirements, it likely doesn't take things into consideration that would satisfy another set of requirements that have not yet been written (nor should it). As such, when requirements change so must the code, and if there are time constraints present then code quality might suffer as a result of cutting corners.

Poorly Designed Architecture

Even if you're aware of what makes a good architecture, it's not always feasible to spend a significant amount of time planning everything out. And if you don't have a clear picture of how everything should work together from the beginning, you may have to do some refactoring down the road. It's also fairly common to build a new feature really quickly (which can result in cutting corners) to see if it gets traction with users and then either clean up the code later if it does or remove it if it doesn't.

Underestimating Difficulty

Estimating how long software development will take is difficult, and unfortunately these estimates are often used to create schedules. When a project's timescale is underestimated it puts pressure on developers to "just get it done," which leads to writing code quickly without putting too much thought into it. If this happens frequently enough even the best code can turn into a big plate of "spaghetti code" that's difficult to understand and unruly to manage.

Ignoring Best Practices

It can be difficult to stay up to date with every best practice, especially if your job encompasses many technologies and/or managing people. If you're working on a team and overlook a best practice, then hopefully you'll have a colleague that will make you aware of it. If the opportunity to use a best practice is missed, then at some point in the future you may have to revisit your code and do some refactoring.

Difficulty Keeping Up with Best Practices

Technology changes at a very rapid pace, and as a result a technique that was once considered a best practice might not be anymore. For example, before 2011 if you wanted to display a container that appeared to have rounded corners on a website, you would need to have an image for each of the corners, embed the images in your HTML, and then position them using CSS to make sure everything lined up correctly. Today this technique is obsolete because modern browsers can display rounded corners with the border-radius CSS property. If you don't continually update your code to make use of modern best practices, over time your technical debt will build up and you'll find your code in a much worse state than it otherwise could be.

When Should Code Be Refactored?

Refactoring code is much easier when it's done with context. As such, it's usually best to refactor when you're fixing a bug or building a new feature that makes use of existing code. Refactoring code consistently while working on smaller tasks reduces the likelihood of breaking anything, and those who modify the same code after it's been refactored will also benefit from your work. Over time, consistent refactoring will lead to superior code, provided your changes align with the properties of good architecture.

However, sometimes you'll run across a piece of code that has a lot of dependencies, and you may be faced with the decision of whether or not you should refactor. Refactoring a piece of code that has a lot of dependencies can be like pulling a loose thread on a shirt: the more you pull the thread, the more it unravels. Similarly, the more you modify a piece of code that has a lot of dependencies, the more dependencies you'll end up having to update. In situations like this, if you're up against a tight deadline it might be beneficial to get your work done in time first, and then allocate some time to go back and refactor. However, if you find along the way that there are smaller things that can be refactored without adversely affecting your schedule, you might consider refactoring them now.

When Should Code NOT Be Refactored?

Knowing when *not* to refactor code is probably even more important than knowing when it should be refactored. Refactoring can have a bad reputation because often software developers seem to rewrite code just for the sake of rewriting it. Maybe someone else wrote the code and the person doing the unnecessary refactoring is suffering from a case of Not Written Here Syndrome, where they feel the code is inferior because they didn't write it. Or perhaps one day someone decides that they just don't like the way they've written code previously (maybe they used underscores instead of dashes in class names and now want to do the opposite), so they embark down the rabbit hole of changing things to scratch this itch. In many cases this can be considered "fake work" that makes people feel productive even when they aren't. In Chapter 5 we'll discuss how to form a plan for how your code should be written by drafting a set of coding standards. At that point it will be much clearer that you should only refactor when doing so will improve your architecture or if it aligns with your coding standards.

Am I Allowed to Refactor My Code?

If you're working on a personal project, then the answer is a resounding "yes!"—but if you're working for an organization where you're not necessarily in charge, the answer might not be as clear. In a perfect world every organization would understand the importance of refactoring, but often that's not the reality. If colleagues in your organization lack technical knowledge about refactoring, you might try to educate them; I hear *CSS Refactoring* books make nice gifts!

Reasonable people that are responsible for ensuring software ships with high-quality code will likely get it, but those that don't may argue that:

- Spending time to rewrite code without seeing changes is a waste of time and money.
- If it's not broken, it doesn't need to be fixed.
- You should have written the code correctly the first time.

If you encounter any of these arguments and you feel confident enough to do so, my advice is to refactor your code anyway, provided you stay on schedule and are careful not to break anything. If you've heard statements like these, I'm willing to bet the person making them has never participated in a code review, so your changes probably won't be noticed anyway. However, if you're refactoring code just for the sake of refactoring, you may consider waiting until it becomes more apparent that the changes will be necessary; premature optimization can often be just as bad as technical debt.

Refactoring Examples

Now that you have a general idea of the benefits of refactoring and when it is (and isn't) a good idea to do it, we can start to talk about how you go about refactoring your code.

Although this book is about refactoring CSS, it's much easier to initially analyze the concept with code that calculates a discrete value as opposed to code that changes the appearance of HTML elements. So, our first example will demonstrate refactoring some basic JavaScript that calculates the total price of an ecommerce order. The second example will refactor some CSS.

Code Examples

Because it can be difficult to understand what's going on in long code passages that span multiple pages and files, smaller pieces of code will be used for examples in this book. All the JavaScript code from our first example can be embedded in an HTML file to make execution easier.

For more complicated examples, CSS that is used to define the general look and feel of the elements in the examples will be included using a separate CSS file.

Styles in this book that are included inline between `<style>` and `</style>` tags will be directly relevant to the example at hand and will be used to illustrate a granular concept.

All code examples are available online at the book's companion website (*https://www.cssrefactoringbook.com*).

Refactoring Example 1: Calculating the Total Price of an Ecommerce Order

Example 1-1 contains some JavaScript that calculates the total price of an ecommerce order if provided with:

- The price of each item purchased
- The quantity of each item purchased
- The cost to ship each item purchased
- The customer's shipping information
- An optional discount code that can reduce the price of the order

Example 1-1. Calculating an ecommerce order total

```
/**
 * Calculates the total order price after shipping costs, discounts, and
 * taxes are applied.
 *
 * @param {Object} customer - a collection of information about
 *    the person that placed the order.
```

```
 *
 * @param {Array.<Object>} lineItems - a collection of products
 *    and quantities being purchased as well as the cost to ship one unit.
 *
 * @param {string} discountCode - an optional discount code that can trigger
 *    a discount to be deducted before shipping and tax are added.
 */
var getOrderTotal = function (customer, lineItems, discountCode) {
  var discountTotal = 0;
  var lineItemTotal = 0;
  var shippingTotal = 0;
  var taxTotal = 0;

  for (var i = 0; i < lineItems.length; i++) {
      var lineItem = lineItems[i];
      lineItemTotal += lineItem.price * lineItem.quantity;
      shippingTotal += lineItem.shippingPrice * lineItem.quantity;
  }

  if (discountCode === '20PERCENT') {
      discountTotal = lineItemTotal * 0.2;
  }

  if (customer.shiptoState === 'CA') {
      taxTotal = (lineItemTotal - discountTotal) * 0.08;
  }

  var total = (
      lineItemTotal -
      discountTotal +
      shippingTotal +
      taxTotal
  );

  return total;
};
```

Calling `getOrderTotal` using the data in Example 1-2 results in `Total: $266` being
printed. Example 1-3 explains why that result is printed.

Example 1-2. Running getOrderTotal with test input

```
var lineItem1 = {
  price: 50,
  quantity: 1,
  shippingPrice: 10
};

var lineItem2 = {
  price: 100,
  quantity: 2,
```

```
  shippingPrice: 20
};

var lineItems = [lineItem1, lineItem2];

var customer = {
  shiptoState: 'CA'
};

var discountCode = '20PERCENT';

var total = getOrderTotal(customer, lineItems, discountCode);

document.writeln('Total: $' + total);
```

Example 1-3. Explanation of why getOrderTotal prints "Total: $266"

```
discountTotal = 0
lineItemTotal = 0
shippingTotal = 0
taxTotal = 0

# FOR LOOP 1st iteration:
lineItemTotal = 0 + (50 * 1) = 50
shippingTotal = 0 + (10 * 1) = 10

# FOR LOOP 2nd iteration:
lineItemTotal = 50 + (100 * 2) = 250
shippingTotal = 10 + (20 * 2) = 50

# discountTotal gets calculated because discountCode equals "20 PERCENT":
discountTotal = 250 * 0.2 = 50

# taxTotal gets set because customer.shiptoState equals "CA":
taxTotal = (250 - 50) * 0.08 = 16

total = 250 - 50 + 50 + 16 = 266
```

Unit tests

After walking through the calculations, the math checks out and everything appears to be working as expected. To ensure that things continue working over time, we can now write a unit test. Put simply, a *unit test* is a piece of code that executes another piece of code to make sure everything is working as expected. Unit tests should be written to test singular pieces of functionality in order to narrow down the root cause of any issues that may surface. Further, a suite of unit tests that are written for your entire project should be run before releasing new code so bugs that have been introduced into the system can be discovered and fixed before it's too late.

The input data from Example 1-2 can be used to write a unit test, shown in Example 1-4, that asserts the function returns the expected value (266). After the test is done running, a count of how many successful and unsuccessful tests were run in addition to a list of unsuccessful tests will be printed.

Example 1-4. A unit test for getOrderTotal

```
var successfulTestCount = 0;
var unsuccessfulTestCount = 0;
var unsuccessfulTestSummaries = [];

/**
 * Asserts the calculations in `getOrdertotal()` are correct.
 */
var testGetOrderTotal = function () {

    // set up expectations

    var expectedTotal = 266;

    // set up test data

    var lineItem1 = {
        price: 50,
        quantity: 1,
        shippingPrice: 10
    };

    var lineItem2 = {
        price: 100,
        quantity: 2,
        shippingPrice: 20
    };

    var lineItems = [lineItem1, lineItem2];

    var customer = {
        shiptoState: 'CA'
    };

    var discountCode = '20PERCENT';

    var total = getOrderTotal(customer, lineItems, discountCode);

    // test the results against expectations

    if (total === expectedTotal) {
      successfulTestCount++;
    } else {
      unsuccessfulTestCount++;
      unsuccessfulTestSummaries.push(
```

```
            'testGetOrderTotal: expected ' + expectedTotal + '; actual ' + total
    );
    }
};

// run tests

testGetOrderTotal();
document.writeln(successfulTestCount + ' successful test(s)<br/>');
document.writeln(unsuccessfulTestCount + ' unsuccessful test(s)<br/>');

if (unsuccessfulTestCount) {
    document.writeln('<ul>');
    for(var i = 0; i < unsuccessfulTestSummaries.length; i++) {
        document.writeln('<li>' + unsuccessfulTestSummaries[i] + '</li>');
    }
    document.writeln('</ul>');
}
```

Executing `testGetOrderTotal` results in the test successfully passing the assertion, as can be seen in Figure 1-1.

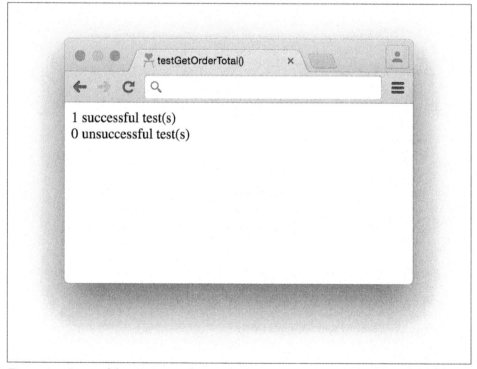

Figure 1-1. Successful unit test results

However, if in the future for some reason a bug was introduced and the multiplier used in the calculation of `discountTotal` changed from 0.2 to –0.2, this would no longer be the case and we would instead see the result pictured in Figure 1-2.

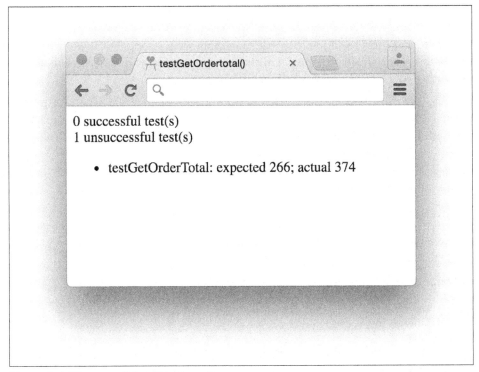

Figure 1-2. Unsuccessful unit test results

Unit tests are a powerful way to ensure that your system continues working as expected over time. They can be especially helpful when rewriting code because an assertion will already be documented, and that assertion will provide greater confidence that the code's behavior hasn't changed.

Now that we understand the code used to calculate the total price of an ecommerce order and we have an accompanying unit test, let's see how refactoring can improve things.

Refactoring getOrderTotal

Looking closely at `getOrderTotal` reveals that there are a number of calculations being performed in that one function:

- The total discount to be subtracted from the final price
- The total price for all of the line items

- The total shipping costs
- The total tax costs
- The total order price

If a bug is accidentally introduced into one of those five calculations, the unit test (testGetOrderTotal) will indicate that something went wrong, but it won't be obvious what *specifically* went wrong. This is the main reason why unit tests should be written to test single pieces of functionality.

To make the code more granular, each of the aforementioned calculations should be extracted into a separate function that has a name describing what it does, like in Example 1-5.

Example 1-5. Extracting code fragments into new functions

```
/**
 * Calculates the total price of all line items ordered.
 *
 * @param {Array.<Object>} lineItems - a collection of products
 *    and quantities being purchased and the cost to ship one unit.
 *
 * @returns {number} The total price of all line items ordered.
 */
var getLineItemTotal = function (lineItems) {
    var lineItemTotal = 0;

    for (var i = 0; i < lineItems.length; i++) {
        var lineItem = lineItems[i];
        lineItemTotal += lineItem.price * lineItem.quantity;
    }


    return lineItemTotal;
};

/**
 * Calculates the total shipping cost of all line items ordered.
 *
 * @param {Array.<Object>} lineItems - a collection of products
 *    and quantities being purchased and the cost to ship one unit.
 *
 * @returns {number} The total price to ship of all line items ordered.
 */
var getShippingTotal = function (lineItems) {
    var shippingTotal = 0;

    for (var i = 0; i < lineItems.length; i++) {
        var lineItem = lineItems[i];
        shippingTotal += lineItem.shippingPrice * lineItem.quantity;
    }
```

```
    return shippingTotal;
};

/**
 * Calculates the total discount to be subtracted from an order total.
 *
 * @param {number} lineItemTotal - The total price of all line items ordered.
 *
 * @param {string} discountCode - An optional discount code that can trigger a
 *    discount to be deducted before shipping and tax are added.
 *
 * @returns {number} The total discount to be subtracted from an order total.
 */
var getDiscountTotal = function (lineItemTotal, discountCode) {
    var discountTotal = 0;

    if (discountCode === '20PERCENT') {
        discountTotal = lineItemTotal * 0.2;
    }

    return discountTotal;
};


/**
 * Calculates the total tax to apply to an order.
 *
 * @param {number} lineItemTotal - The total price of all line items ordered.
 *
 * @param {Object} customer - A collection of information about the person that
 *    placed an order.
 *
 * @returns {number} The total tax to be applied to an order.
 */
var getTaxTotal = function () {
    var taxTotal = 0;

    if (customer.shiptoState === 'CA') {
        taxTotal = lineItemTotal * 0.08;
    }

    return taxTotal;
};
```

Each new function should also have an accompanying unit test like the one in Example 1-6.

Example 1-6. Unit tests for extracted functions written in JavaScript

```javascript
/**
 * Asserts getLineItemTotal works as expected.
 */
var testGetLineItemTotal = function () {
    var lineItem1 = {
        price: 50,
        quantity: 1
    };

    var lineItem2 = {
        price: 100,
        quantity: 2
    };

    var lineItemTotal = getLineItemTotal([lineItem1, lineItem2]);
    var expectedTotal = 250;

    if (lineItemTotal === expectedTotal) {
      successfulTestCount++;
    } else {
      unsuccessfulTestCount++;
      unsuccessfulTestSummaries.push(
          'testGetLineItemTotal: expected ' + expectedTotal + '; actual ' +
          lineItemTotal
      );
    }
};

/**
 * Asserts getShippingTotal works as expected.
 */
var testGetShippingTotal = function () {
    var lineItem1 = {
        quantity: 1,
        shippingPrice: 10
    };

    var lineItem2 = {
        quantity: 2,
        shippingPrice: 20
    };

    var shippingTotal = getShippingTotal([lineItem1, lineItem2]);
    var expectedTotal = 250;

    if (shippingTotal === expectedTotal) {
      successfulTestCount++;
    } else {
      unsuccessfulTestCount++;
      unsuccessfulTestSummaries.push(
```

```
            'testGetShippingTotal: expected ' + expectedTotal + '; actual ' +
            shippingTotal
        );
    }
};

/**
 * Ensures GetDiscountTotal works as expected when a valid discount code
 * is used.
 */
var testGetDiscountTotalWithValidDiscountCode = function () {
    var discountTotal = getDiscountTotal(100, '20PERCENT');
    var expectedTotal = 20;

    if (discountTotal === expectedTotal) {
      successfulTestCount++;
    } else {
      unsuccessfulTestCount++;
      unsuccessfulTestSummaries.push(
          'testGetDiscountTotalWithValidDiscountCode: expected ' + expectedTotal +
          '; actual ' + discountTotal
      );
    }
};

/**
 * Ensures GetDiscountTotal works as expected when an invalid discount code
 * is used.
 */
var testGetDiscountTotalWithInvalidDiscountCode = function () {
    var discountTotal = get_discount_total(100, '90PERCENT');
    var expectedTotal = 0;

    if (discountTotal === expectedTotal) {
      successfulTestCount++;
    } else {
      unsuccessfulTestCount++;
      unsuccessfulTestSummaries.push(
          'testGetDiscountTotalWithInvalidDiscountCode: expected ' + expectedTotal +
          '; actual ' + discountTotal
      );
    }
};

/**
 * Ensures GetTaxTotal works as expected when the customer lives in California.
 */
var testGetTaxTotalForCaliforniaResident = function () {
    var customer = {
      shiptoState: 'CA'
    };
```

```
    var taxTotal = getTaxTotal(100, customer);
    var expectedTotal = 8;

    if (taxTotal === expectedTotal) {
      successfulTestCount++;
    } else {
      unsuccessfulTestCount++;
      unsuccessfulTestSummaries.push(
          'testGetTaxTotalForCaliforniaResident: expected ' + expectedTotal +
          '; actual ' + taxTotal
      );
    }
};

/**
 * Ensures GetTaxTotal works as expected when the customer doesn't live
 * in California.
 */
var testGetTaxTotalForNonCaliforniaResident = function () {
    var customer = {
        shiptoState: 'MA'
    };

    var taxTotal = getTaxTotal(100, customer);
    var expectedTotal = 0;

    if (taxTotal === expectedTotal) {
      successfulTestCount++;
    } else {
      unsuccessfulTestCount++;
      unsuccessfulTestSummaries.push(
          'testGetTaxTotalForNonCaliforniaResident: expected ' + expectedTotal +
          '; actual ' + taxTotal
      );
    }
};
```

Finally, `getOrderTotal` should be modified to make use of the new functions, as seen in Example 1-7.

Example 1-7. Modifying getOrderTotal to use extracted functions

```
/**
 * Calculates the total order price after shipping costs, discounts, and
 * taxes are applied.
 *
 * @param {Object} customer - a collection of information about
 *    the person that placed the order.
 *
 * @param {Array.<Object>} lineItems - a collection of products
 *    and quantities being purchased and the cost to ship one unit.
```

```
 *
 * @param {string} discountCode - an optional discount code that can trigger
 *   a discount to be deducted before shipping and tax are added.
 */
var getOrderTotal = function (customer, lineItems, discountCode) {
    var lineItemTotal = getLineItemTotal(lineItems);
    var shippingTotal = getShippingTotal(lineItems);
    var discountTotal = getDiscountTotal(lineItemTotal, discountCode);
    var taxTotal = getTaxTotal(lineTtemTotal, customer);

    return lineItemTotal - discountTotal + shippingTotal + taxTotal;
};
```

After analyzing the preceding code, the following observations can be made:

- There are more functions than before.
- There are more unit tests than before.
- Each function does one particular thing.
- Each function has an accompanying unit test.
- Functions can be used together to perform more complex calculations.

Overall, this code is in much better shape now. The individual calculations used in getOrderTotal have been extracted and each has an accompanying unit test. This means that it will be much easier to pinpoint exactly which piece of functionality is broken should a bug be introduced into the code. Additionally, if the totals for tax or shipping needed to be calculated in another piece of code, the existing functionality that already has unit tests can be used.

Refactoring Example 2: A Simple Example of Refactoring CSS

Example 1-8 is some code that displays the headline of a website.

Example 1-8. HTML for a website headline

```
<!doctype html>
<html>
  <head>
    <title>Ferguson's Cat Shelter</title>
    <link rel="stylesheet" type="text/css" href="css/style.css" />
  </head>
  <body>
    <main>
      <h1 style="font-family: Helvetica, Arial, sans-serif;font-size: 36px;
        font-weight: 400;text-align: center;">
        San Francisco's Premiere Cat Shelter
      </h1>
    </main>
```

```
    </body>
</html>
```

Opening up a browser and loading *index.html* will display Figure 1-3.

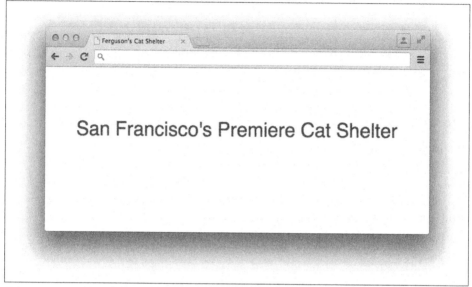

Figure 1-3. Screenshot of website headline

In our first refactoring example we wrote a unit test for the code before refactoring to ensure its behavior didn't change. When refactoring CSS it's still important to make sure that your modifications don't change anything, but unfortunately it's not as straightforward because something visual is being tested rather than something that produces discrete values. Chapter 5 discusses useful techniques for maintaining visual equality. For now, though, simply taking a screenshot to provide a visual reference before refactoring will suffice.

Refactoring the website headline

Looking at the code in Example 1-8, it's clear that there's room for improvement because the headline, denoted by an <h1> tag, has its styles embedded in the style attribute. When styles are embedded in HTML via an element's style attribute or between <style></style> tags, they are known as *inline styles*.

Much like the original function in Example 1-1 that performed multiple calculations, inline styles are not very reusable. When styles are set using the style attribute, they can only be applied to that particular element. When styles are embedded between <style></style> tags, they can only be applied to that particular page.

Because most websites have multiple pages that could each have a headline, these styles should be extracted out of the HTML into a separate CSS file (in this case *style.css*) that can be included on multiple pages and cached by the browser. The contents of *style.css* are depicted in Example 1-9, and Example 1-10 shows the HTML with the inline CSS extracted.

Example 1-9. Headline CSS extracted into style.css

```
h1 {
  font-family: Helvetica, Arial, sans-serif;
  font-size: 36px;
  font-weight: 400;
  text-align: center;
}
```

Example 1-10. HTML with inline CSS extracted

```
<!doctype html>
<html>
  <head>
    <title>Ferguson's Cat Shelter</title>
    <link rel="stylesheet" type="text/css" href="css/style.css" />
  </head>
  <body>
    <main>
      <h1>San Francisco's Premiere Cat Shelter</h1>
    </main>
  </body>
</html>
```

A quick browser refresh shows that nothing has changed, and once again some observations can be made:

- Extracting inline CSS promotes reusability.
- Separating functionality (styles and structure) makes code more readable.
- Regression testing can be performed manually in a web browser or by comparing a refactored interface against a screenshot.

Extracting styles into a separate file promotes code reuse because those styles can be used across multiple pages. When CSS is in a file separate from HTML, both the HTML and the CSS are easier to read because the HTML does not have extremely long lines of style definitions in it, and the CSS is grouped together in logical chunks. Finally, testing of changes can be performed by manually reloading the page in the browser so the changes can be compared against a screenshot that was taken before refactoring.

Although this example was very simple, lots of small changes like this can produce a sizable benefit over time.

Chapter Summary

We've made it through the first chapter, and we know what refactoring is and how it relates to software architecture. We also learned why refactoring is important and when it should be performed. Finally, we walked through two refactoring examples and learned about unit tests. Next, we'll learn about the cascade, which is arguably the most important concept to understand when it comes to writing CSS.

CHAPTER 2

Understanding the Cascade

There's nothing worse than writing a bunch of CSS only to test it out and find that other styles are being applied instead of the ones you intended. To better understand why this happens, this chapter explains how web browsers determine which styles to apply to which elements using the cascade.

What Is the Cascade?

The *cascade* is the method by which the browser determines how styles should be applied to elements. Because multiple styles can be applied to the same element, understanding how the cascade works is important in the event that styles are not applied they way you expect them to be. Luckily, it's not as complicated as it sounds; styles are applied based on the specificity of their selectors as well as the order in which they appear.

Selector Specificity

Specificity is a measure of how precisely elements are identified based on the CSS selectors used. Specificity is calculated by analyzing the different types of selectors (except the universal selector, `*`) that are combined to select an element. A specificity is determined by plugging numbers into (`a`, `b`, `c`, `d`):

1. If the styles are applied via the `style` attribute, `a`=1; otherwise, `a`=0.

2. `b` is equal to the number of ID selectors present.

3. `c` is equal to the number of class selectors, attribute selectors, and pseudoclasses present.

4. `d` is equal to the number of type selectors and pseudoelements present.

When all of these calculations are completed, those numbers are concatenated to give the specificity. To make this a bit more concrete, consider the selector in Example 2-1.

Example 2-1. An example ruleset to calculate specificity for

```
#nav-global > ul > li > a.nav-link {
    color: #000000;
}
```

Using the algorithm just defined, we can determine that this selector has a specificity of (0,1,1,3):

1. The styles are not applied via the `style` attribute, so a=0
2. There is 1 ID selector (`#nav-global`), so b=1
3. There is 1 class selector (`.nav-link`), so c=1
4. there are 3 type selectors (`ul`, `li`, and `a`), so d=3

When comparing the specificity of selectors, the selector that has the largest number farthest to the left has the highest specificity. If the two leftmost numbers being compared are equal, then the next number to the left is used, and so on. For example, a specificity of (1, 0, 0, 0) is higher than (0, 1, 1, 3), in the same way (0, 2, 1, 3) is higher than (0, 1, 1, 3). However, a specificity of (0, 1, 1, 3) is lower than a specificity of (0, 1, 1, 4) or (0, 1, 2, 0). Example 2-2 gives some more examples of calculating specificity.

Example 2-2. Examples of calculating specificity

```
/**
 * This selector has a specificity of (0,0,2,2) because there are:
 *   0 inline styles
 *   0 IDs
 *   1 class (.title), 0 attribute selectors, and 1 pseudoclass (:first-child)
 *   2 type selectors (li, h2)
 */
li:first-child h2 .title {}

/**
 * This selector has a specificity of (0,1,2,1) because there are:
 *   0 inline styles
 *   1 ID (#nav)
 *   1 class (.selected), 0 attribute selectors, and 1 pseudoclass (:hover)
 *   1 type selector (a)
 */
#nav .selected > a:hover {}

/**
 * This selector has a specificity of (0,1,2,3) because there are:
 *   0 inline styles
```

```
 *    1 ID (#nav)
 *    1 class (.selected), 0 attribute selectors, and 1 pseudoclass (:hover)
 *    3 type selectors  (html, body, a)
 */
html body #nav .selected > a:hover {}
```

Ruleset Order

Ruleset order describes the location of a CSS ruleset in a stylesheet. When two declaration blocks that have selectors of equal specificity attempt to style a property on the
same element, the properties in the declaration block that appears later in the stylesheet have precedence. This means that the `color` property for the element styled in
Example 2-3 is assigned the value `#000000` because a declaration block with the same
specificity appears later in the stylesheet and assigns that color.

Example 2-3. Assigning a value to the color property with a later declaration block

```
<!doctype html>
<html>
  <head>
    <title>Inline Styles and Specificity</title>
    <style type="text/css">
      #nav-global > ul > li > a.nav-link {
        color: #FFFFFF;
      }
      #nav-global > ul > li > a.nav-link {
        color: #000000;
      }
    </style>
  </head>
  <body>
    <nav id="nav-global">
      <ul>
        <li>
          <a href="#" class="nav-link">Link</a>
        </li>
      </ul>
    </nav>
  </body>
</html>
```

Inline CSS and Specificity

Specificity and ruleset order are paramount in determining how styles are applied to
an element, unless it has inline styles applied via the `style` attribute. In Example 2-4
there are inline styles present on the anchor tag. Because the `color` property is being
set on the actual element, that style will be applied. No matter how specific the selec-

tor is in either a `<style>` block or an external stylesheet, it will never be more specific than styles on the actual element.

Example 2-4. Assigning a value to the color property with inline CSS via the style attribute

```html
<!doctype html>
<html>
  <head>
    <title>Inline Styles and Specificity</title>
    <style type="text/css">
      #nav-global > ul > li > a.nav-link {
        color: #000000;
      }
    </style>
  </head>
  <body>
    <nav id="nav-global">
      <ul>
        <li>
          <a href="/" class="nav-link" style="color: #1200FF;">Link</a>
        </li>
      </ul>
    </nav>
  </body>
</html>
```

Overriding the Cascade with the !important Declaration

The only way to ensure that styles present in a `<style>` block or an external stylesheet are more specific than any other styles (including inline styles applied with the `style` attribute) is to append `!important` to a declaration. When `!important` is appended to a declaration, it indicates to the browser that that declaration should be used for elements that match its containing ruleset's selectors, regardless of the properties applied by selectors that have a higher specificity. When multiple declaration blocks that select the same elements make use of `!important`, the one that appears last is applied.

In Example 2-5, for instance, the anchor tag appears with white (#FFFFFF) text because the `!important` declaration is used in the first ruleset. If `!important` was used in both rulesets, the anchor tag would have black (#000000) text because that ruleset appears last. If `!important` was not used at all, the anchor tag would have blue (#1200FF) text because inline styles have the highest specificity. Note that `!important` cannot be used on styles applied with the `style` attribute (i.e., `<a href="/" style="color: #1200FF !important">Link</a>`).

Example 2-5. Assigning a value to the color property with an earlier declaration block using !important

```
<!doctype html>
<html>
  <head>
    <title>Inline Styles and Specificity</title>
    <style type="text/css">
      #nav-global > ul > li > a.nav-link {
        color: #FFFFFF !important;
      }
      #nav-global > ul > li > a.nav-link {
        color: #000000;
      }
    </style>
  </head>
  <body>
    <nav id="nav-global">
      <ul>
        <li>
          <a href="/" class="nav-link" style="color: #1200FF;">Link</a>
        </li>
      </ul>
    </nav>
  </body>
</html>
```

Chapter Summary

With a solid understanding of the cascade and how to calculate specificity, learning more about refactoring will be a bit easier because it all hinges on these ideas. In the coming chapters, be sure to think about how the cascade plays into each concept and it will become much more apparent how everything is tied together. Next, we'll shift gears a bit and look at some recommendations for how to write better CSS.

CHAPTER 3

Writing Better CSS

"Best practices" is a contentious term when it comes to writing CSS because there are so many different ways to accomplish the same thing, and the preference for one technique over another can be very subjective. However, as Chapter 1 explained, a good architecture is predictable, maintainable, extensible, and promotes code reuse. The ideas presented in the following sections keep this definition in mind and are intended to provide a solid foundation from which you can write better CSS.

Use Comments

Comments provide documentation that is helpful when looking at a file in the future. Comments should be used to document things including:

- File contents
- Selectors' dependencies, usages, etc.
- Why certain declarations were used (this is especially helpful in regard to browser quirks)
- Deprecated styles that are being refactored and should no longer be used

CSS only has block-level comments (comments that can span multiple lines), and they begin with /* and end with */. In the event that a comment only needs one line, that can be done, but it must still begin with /* and end with */. Here are some examples of comments:

```
/*
 * Styles for main navigation links.
 *
 * @see templates/_navigation.html
 */
```

```css
.nav-link {
  padding: 4px;
  text-decoration: none;
}

.nav-link:hover {
  border-bottom: 4px solid #000000;

  /*
   * prevents addition of the 4px bottom border
   * from making the element shift
   */
  padding-bottom: 0;
}

/* @deprecated */
.navigation-link {
  color: #1200FF;
}
```

Consistently Structure Rulesets

Rulesets can be written all on one line or they can be formatted to use multiple lines. Example 3-1 shows what a ruleset looks like on one line, and Example 3-2 shows what it looks like on multiple lines. Rulesets can even have their curly braces on new lines, as seen in Example 3-3.

Example 3-1. CSS ruleset on one line

```css
selector { property1: value; property2: value; property3: value; }
```

Example 3-2. CSS ruleset on multiple lines

```css
selector {
    property1: value;
    property2: value;
    property3: value;
}
```

Example 3-3. CSS ruleset with braces on multiple lines

```css
selector
{
    property1: value;
    property2: value;
    property3: value;
}
```

Writing rulesets consistently makes your CSS more predictable, which in turn makes it easier to understand.

While it's certainly a matter of preference, my preference is for each ruleset to have each declaration on its own line like in Example 3-2. Additionally, I like keeping CSS properties in alphabetical order; this makes things even more predictable by making it easier to find any given property.

Organize Properties with Vendor Prefixes

A *vendor prefix* is a string that browser makers prepend to new and experimental CSS properties before their behavior is standardized. Typically the prefixes are `-webkit-` for browsers that use the Blink or WebKit rendering engines (Chrome and Safari), `-moz-` for browsers that use the Gecko rendering engine (Firefox), and `-ms-` for browsers that use the Trident rendering engine (Internet Explorer/Edge). When a property is standardized there is no prefix appended to it.

For example, `transform-origin` is one such property. `transform-origin` allows you to modify the origin at which transformations (like rotations and translations) occur on elements. In order to use it today, vendor prefixes should be used with the standardized version as a fallback:

```
-ms-transform-origin: @origin;
-moz-transform-origin: @origin;
-webkit-transform-origin: @origin;
transform-origin: @origin;
```

The order of these properties is very important because as the browser applies properties in a declaration block from top to bottom, it ignores the ones it does not recognize and applies the ones it does. This means that placing a non-prefixed standard CSS property before its vendor-prefixed version could result in it being overridden on browsers that support both.

Old browsers that do not support a new property or any of its vendor-prefixed versions will simply ignore them. Other old browsers that only support the vendor-prefixed version of the new property will apply the appropriate one and ignore the standard non-prefixed version. Newer browsers that continue to support the vendor-prefixed version of a new property for backward compatibility, but also support the standard non-prefixed version, can apply both. Finally, modern browsers that have dropped support for the vendor-prefixed version of a property and only support the standard non-prefixed version will ignore the vendor-prefixed version and apply the standard version.

Since it may take some time for all users of a particular browser to upgrade, both the prefixed and unprefixed properties should remain until that browser is no longer supported by your website.

Feature Flags

Vendor-prefixed CSS properties can be burdensome to maintain because they notoriously bloat stylesheets. To combat this, many browser makers have made the switch to using opt-in features so developers can experiment with bleeding-edge CSS properties. If your website is still visited by people using older browsers and you need to support them, however, you may want to continue to maintain those vendor-prefixed CSS properties.

Keep Selectors Simple

Selectors can be made very complex by stringing lots of different selectors and combinators together. However, just because selectors can be very specific doesn't mean they should be. Consider the code in Example 3-4.

Example 3-4. CSS that selects a very specific element

```
<!doctype html>
<html>
  <head>
    <title>Keep Selectors Simple</title>
    <style type="text/css">
      div > nav > ul > li > a {
          color: #1200FF;
      }
    </style>
  </head>
  <body>
    <div>
      <nav>
        <ul>
          <li>
            <a href="./policies.html">Policies</a>
          </li>
        </ul>
      </nav>
    </div>
  </body>
</html>
```

The code in Example 3-4 styles a very particular anchor tag because of its use of multiple child combinators (>). This isn't a great way to style the anchor tag element because the selector being used is highly dependent on the HTML structure present on the page. Should something change within that HTML structure, the desired styles will no longer be applied. Instead, adding a class to the HTML element and styling that class is a better solution, as illustrated in Example 3-5.

Example 3-5. HTML hierarchy with an added class

```
<!doctype html>
<html>
  <head>
    <title>Keep Selectors Simple</title>
    <style type="text/css">
      a.nav-link {
          color: #1200FF;
      }
    </style>
  </head>
  <body>
    <div>
      <nav>
        <ul>
          <li>
            <a href="./policies.html" class="nav-link">Policies</a>
          </li>
        </ul>
      </nav>
    </div>
  </body>
</html>
```

Now that all of the complicated child selectors have been removed, in Example 3-5 the class selector is used to select elements with the class nav-link. However, the selector a.nav-link is still more specific than it needs to be: it's said to be an *overqualified selector* because it can only be used on anchor tags.

As can be seen in Example 3-6, the selector can be simplified further.

Example 3-6. A simplified selector

```
.nav-link {
  color: #1200FF;
}
```

Simplifying the selector as much as possible, as shown here, is beneficial because it means these styles are no longer dependent on the HTML structure being used and the CSS file size will be slightly smaller. Should this element need to be styled differently than it is in Example 3-6, this can be done in in relation to its parent container (e.g., .parent-container .nav-link { color: #FF0000; }), which not only styles the element differently, but also provides context for when those styles should apply.

However, there are times when qualifying selectors *is* appropriate—for example, when applying a class to one element results in a different behavior than it would when applied to a different element.

In Example 3-7, the error class makes text red. When styling inputs, though, the design might call for both the text and the border to be red without changing the styles of other elements that share the error class. Because input.error is as specific as it needs to be to style an input element's text and border color, it is considered a *qualified selector* as opposed to an overqualified selector.

Example 3-7. Acceptable qualified selectors

```
.error {
  color: #FF0000;
}

input.error {
  border-color: #FF0000;
}
```

Performant Selectors

Less complex selectors are more performant than complicated selectors; however, as computers continue to get faster and browsers continue to be optimized, most of the time selector performance shouldn't be something to stress out about. Simple selectors should be preferred because they are more reusable and easy to understand, not because they are noticeably more efficient. Following the guidelines in this book should help you avoid selector performance anxiety, but having a general idea of how selectors work is still worthwhile.

Matching selectors from right to left

Web browsers need to be able to select elements and apply styles quickly so the web page can be used as soon as possible. The browser matches selectors from right to left so it can eliminate elements that don't match up front, rather than wasting time checking elements that *might* match. To illustrate this concept, take a look at Example 3-8, which contains some markup that houses a .nav-link and a strong element.

Example 3-8. A simple HTML hierarchy

```
<!doctype html>
<html>
  <head>
    <title>Another Example</title>
  </head>
  <body>
    <div>
      <nav>
        <ul>
          <li>
```

```
          <strong>Not a Link</strong>
        </li>
      </ul>
    </nav>
  </div>
  <div>
    <nav>
      <ul>
        <li>
          <a href="#" class="nav-link">Link</a>
        </li>
      </ul>
    </nav>
  </div>
  </body>
</html>
```

If the anchor tag is selected using the selector div > nav > ul > li > a and the browser tried to match elements (excluding <!doctype>) from left to right, it would need to:

1. Iterate through each element to see if it is a <div> element.

2. Check each <div> that was matched in step 1 to see if it has a <nav> element as a child.

3. Check each <nav> element that was matched in step 2 to see if it has a <ul> element as a child.

4. Check each <ul> element that was matched in step 3 to see if it has an <li> element as a child.

5. Check each <li> element that was matched in step 4 to see if it has an <a> element as a child.

6. Apply the styles to the one <a> element that was found.

On the other hand, if the same selector (div > nav > ul > li > a) is matched from right to left the browser will need to:

1. Iterate through each element to see if it is an <a> element.

2. Check if each <a> element matched in step 1 has an <li> element as a parent.

3. Check if each <li> element matched in step 2 has a <ul> element as a parent.

4. Check if each <ul> element matched in step 3 has a <nav> element as a parent.

5. Check if each <nav> element matched in step 4 has a <div> element as a parent.

6. Apply the styles to the <a> element that matches the selector.

While the number of steps is the same, the big difference is that when matching the selector from left to right both <div> elements need to be traversed. By matching the selector from right to left the browser is able to eliminate entire hierarchies of elements that do not contain an anchor tag. To make things even more performant the anchor tag can be selected by its class, .nav-link, so all the browser has to do is iterate through each element and check if it has that class.

With this very general understanding of how browsers parse selectors, we can analyze a more extreme (and easy-to-avoid) example.

The key selector

The code in Example 3-9 selects any element that is an ancestor of the <body> tag. Parsing the selector from right to left effectively selects each element on the page and traverses its ancestors to see if one is the <body> tag. This is extremely inefficient because almost every visible element is a descendant of the <body> element.

Example 3-9. Universal selector ancestor example

```
body * {
  font-size: 12px;
}
```

As previously described, the browser will match elements from right to left so it can eliminate elements that don't match the selector sooner rather than later. The rightmost part of a selector is known as the *key selector*, so in Example 3-9 this makes the universal selector * the key selector.

When the universal selector is used by itself to apply styles to all elements (* {}), the browser can do so fairly quickly because it only has to match every element on the page. However, when the universal selector is used in conjunction with another selector and a combinator (the ancestor combinator in Example 3-9), the browser will have to do much more work to match the appropriate elements. This can be avoided by only using the universal selector by itself rather than with combinators and other selectors.

Decouple CSS and JavaScript

JavaScript and CSS can become intertwined because both depend on the classes and IDs that are present on HTML elements. Additionally, because JavaScript can modify an HTML element's styles it can be easy for the responsibilities of these two languages to become muddled. In order to separate the concerns of CSS and JavaScript, classes and IDs used to select elements in JavaScript should not be used to style elements. Similarly, when element styles need to be modified by JavaScript it should be done by adding and removing classes.

Prefix Classes and IDs that Are Used in JavaScript

It's fairly common to find HTML that includes classes that are not only used to style elements with CSS, but also used by JavaScript as selectors. It's also fairly common to see classes and IDs added to elements that are only intended to be used to select elements with no intention of styling them. Classes and IDs that are present in HTML but not used in CSS can make it more difficult to find the styles that are needed to change the appearance of an element. Similarly, JavaScript can break if a class name is changed to more accurately reflect what is being styled without the change to the class name also being made in JavaScript.

A simple fix for this is to prepend the names of classes and IDs that are only intended to be used for JavaScript with `js-`. For example, if a tab group related to policies needed to be selected in JavaScript, the ID `js-tab-group-policies` might be used. By only using classes and IDs that are prepended with `js-` for JavaScript selectors, any dependencies that may exist between JavaScript and CSS can be eliminated.

Modify Element Styles with Classes

Element styles can be modified by JavaScript, and many libraries (like jQuery) make it fairly trivial. However, changing styles in JavaScript usually means adding inline styles to an element via its `style` attribute, which makes those styles among the most specific. Additionally, modifying styles in JavaScript means that the JavaScript is aware of specific CSS styles, which seems to be out of the scope of its responsibility. In the event that the styling of an element needs to be changed, not only will CSS files need to be searched for existing styles, but JavaScript files will also need to be included in that search.

Instead of modifying the styles of an HTML element by adding them to its `style` attribute with JavaScript, classes should be added to or removed from the element. Not only will the appropriate styles be applied, but the CSS rulesets used will continue to be appropriately organized with the rest of the website's CSS.

Use Classes

Classes and IDs are an easy means to identify elements in the DOM that should have certain styles applied to them. Classes can be reused as many times as needed on a page, and they have a fairly low specificity so they can be overridden easily. IDs, on the other hand, are almost exactly the opposite; they have a very high specificity, so they cannot be easily overridden and they should be used at most once per page. When writing CSS for a website that is ever-changing, elements should be styled by using classes.

Exclusively using classes is one of many ideas that divide frontend developers. One argument against only using classes is that IDs are not only valid, but helpful in enforcing that some HTML constructs are only used once. For example, if a website is built that has a two-column page wherein one column is a sidebar and the other houses the page content, the following selectors might be used:

```
#content {
    /* #content styles go here */
}
#sidebar {
    /* #sidebar styles go here */
}
```

The use of IDs implies that these elements will each be used at most once on the page. However, what if at some point the page needs to be modified so the content is displayed between two identically styled sidebars? Either the second sidebar would need new CSS that gets applied with a new ID or class, or `#sidebar` could be changed to use a class so its styles can be reused.

Elements that would benefit from using a unique ID can make use of a unique class name instead, and the same goal can be achieved. If it turns out in the future that that styling needs to be reused, it can be without change. Realistically, in most cases there isn't even a noticeable performance difference between using classes and IDs in regard to CSS.

 IDs are the fastest way to select elements in JavaScript, and not using them to style elements is another good way to decouple CSS from JavaScript, much like prefixing classes and IDs with `js-`.

Assign Classes Meaningful Names

Meaningful class names provide context by expressing what is being styled without giving so little detail that it's ambiguous, but also without giving so much detail that it hinders code reuse.

In Example 3-10 a class is used to select an element, but what is `a`? Cryptic class names are confusing. Maybe `.a` is intended to signify "animal." If so, that would have been a better choice, because `.animal` explains exactly what the element is intended to represent.

Example 3-10. A declaration block with a cryptic class name

```
.a {
  width: 200px;
}
```

However, while it's important to be descriptive, it's just as important not to overdo it. What if instead of `animal`, the class name was `female-black-and-white-kitten`? Technically it could be reused, but this class name is far too specific because other animals might be displayed using the same styles, and this class name might not accurately describe the animals being displayed. `.animal` is a much better class name because it's descriptive enough that it's easy to understand what is being styled, but it's also generic enough that it can describe any type of animal that should be styled similarly, be it male or female, young or old, or an animal that's not a kitten.

Avoid Over-Modularized Classes

Meaningful class names describe the element that is being styled rather than describing the styles being applied to the element. Have you ever seen a piece of HTML that looks like Example 3-11?

Example 3-11. Over-modularized classes

```
<h1 class="font-bold uppercase blue-text margin-bottom-large no-padding">
  Too Many CSS Classes
</h1>
```

These classes describe *how* the element is being styled rather than *what* is being styled. Additionally, these classes are said to be suffering from *over-modularization*—because each class only applies one style, they will always need to be used together. Over-modularized classes should be avoided because they aren't much better than using inline styles, like in Example 3-12.

Example 3-12. Inline CSS

```
<h2 style="font-weight: bold; text-transform: uppercase; color: #1200FF;
 margin-bottom: 20px; padding: 0">
  Too Many CSS Classes
</h2>
```

Instead these styles should be grouped together using a meaningful class name that describes what is being styled, like in Example 3-13. Once that is done, the HTML is much more readable because it is styled using one succinct class name, like in Example 3-14.

Example 3-13. A class that describes what is being styled

```
.section-title {
  color: #1200FF;
  font-weight: bold;
  margin-bottom: 20px;
  padding: 0;
```

```
    text-transform: uppercase;
}
```

Example 3-14. A class that groups over-modularized classes together

```
<h2 class="section-title">
  Too Many CSS Classes
</h2>
```

Build a Better Box

The *box model* is the method by which a browser determines how to render a rectangle. It is important to understand how the box model works because all HTML elements are essentially boxes, and this knowledge can be the difference between everything fitting together properly or not.

Figure 3-1 displays an element that has a set width, height, padding, margin, and border (the color coding for `margin` and `padding` are purely illustrative). This box can be generated using the code in Example 3-15.

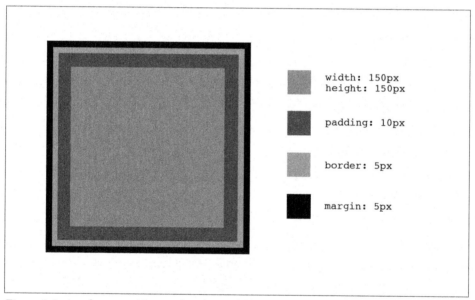

Figure 3-1. An element with a set height, width, padding, margin, and border

Example 3-15. Code for the box in Figure 3-1

```
<!doctype html>
<html>
  <head>
    <title>Determining Dimensions with the Box Model</title>
```

```
<style type="text/css">
  .example-element {
    background-color: #FF0000;
    border: 5px solid #000000;
    display: block;
    height: 150px;
    margin: 5px;
    padding: 10px;
    width: 150px;
  }
</style>
</head>
<body>
  <div class="example-element"></div>
</body>
</html>
```

The dimensions for this box can be calculated in one of two ways, depending on the value assigned to the element's box-sizing property. In each of the following scenarios margin will affect the spacing around the box, but it is not taken into consideration when calculating its size.

box-sizing: content-box

When the box-sizing property is assigned the value content-box, the dimensions of the box are calculated by adding the padding and border dimensions to the element's height and width dimensions. For example, if the dimensions of the box in Figure 3-1 are calculated this way, the box's computed dimensions will be 180 px tall by 180 px wide because:

```
    150px height
  + 10px padding-top
  + 10px padding-bottom
  + 5px border-top
  + 5px border-bottom = 180px computed height

    150px width
  + 10px padding-left
  + 10px padding-right
  + 5px border-left
  + 5px border-right = 180px computed width
```

box-sizing: border-box

When the box-sizing property is assigned the value border-box, the dimensions of the box are based solely on the box's width and height properties. This means that despite the padding and border applied to the box in Figure 3-1, the computed dimensions of the box will be 150 px tall by 150 px wide because those are the dimensions set for the height and width properties; the browser will take padding and border into account and resize the `height` and `width` properties appropriately, so the total dimensions equal those set by the `height` and `width` properties. In this case:

```
    150px computed height
  - 10px padding-top
  - 10px padding-bottom
  -  5px border-top
  -  5px border-bottom = 120px implicit height

    150px computed width
  - 10px padding-left
  - 10px padding-right
  -  5px border-left
  -  5px border-right = 120px implicit width
```

content-box or border-box?

Given that there are two different ways to calculate the dimensions of a box, it's reasonable to wonder which should be used and when. Neither `content-box` nor `border-box` is "better" than the other, but many find `border-box` to be a bit more intuitive as it describes the total height and width of an element from border to border, rather than just the dimensions of the content.

`box-sizing` can be set on any element, so it is possible to mix and match when `border-box` and `content-box` are used, but for consistency's sake it's usually preferable to choose one and stick with it. This can be accomplished by setting the appropriate value using the universal selector:

```
*,
*:after,
*:before {
  box-sizing: border-box;
}
```

Chapter Summary

The concepts in this chapter have laid another piece of the groundwork for when we begin refactoring. Understanding how to write better CSS before we refactor will make refactoring much easier. Next we'll explore the intentions that styles can have and how they can help with code reuse. When reading the next chapter, keep the ideas from this chapter in mind because they will help you make decisions that can simplify your CSS tremendously.

CHAPTER 4

Classifying Different Types of Styles

Code reuse is one of the tenets of good architecture and arguably one of the most important parts of writing high-quality CSS. This chapter discusses the subtle intents that different styles can have when they are applied to HTML elements in logical and deliberate ways. When styles are classified and used in relation to their intent, finding ways to reuse code becomes much more obvious. As you make your way through this chapter, think back to Chapter 2 and you'll see how classifying different styles parallels how the cascade works.

The Importance of Classifying Styles

At its most basic, a website is a collection of documents that display information. However, on the other end of the spectrum and at its most complicated, a website can more resemble an intricate application that facilitates simple human interactions and enables complex operations. Both of these extremes make use of semantic HTML tags that help describe what is being displayed, and both can benefit from intent-based styling.

Intent-based styling helps create a better architecture because organizing styles into different classifications promotes more predictable code that can be reused more easily. Following are the various classifications of styles that can be applied to any website, despite its intricacies.

Normalizing Styles

Browsers come with a default stylesheet, called the *user agent stylesheet*, that applies default styles to HTML elements. Because different browsers are made by different companies, there can be discrepancies in which properties and values these stylesheets set.

Normalizing styles are styles whose intent is to provide default values for properties on various elements that might otherwise have different defaults across browsers. For example, Example 4-1 normalizes the styling of <hr> elements in various browsers.

Example 4-1. Normalizing <hr> elements across browsers

```
/**
 * 1. Add the correct box sizing in Firefox.
 * 2. Show the overflow in Edge and IE.
 */

hr {
  box-sizing: content-box; /* 1 */
  height: 0; /* 1 */
  overflow: visible; /* 2 */
}
```

It can be difficult to test and keep track of which browsers set which properties and values by default, but luckily the web development community has done much of this work for us already and there are a number of different sets of open source normalizing styles available. One of the most commonly used (and the source of the CSS from Example 4-1) is *normalize.css*, authored by Nicolas Gallagher and Jonathan Neal; it's available on GitHub (*http://necolas.github.io/normalize.css*) and reprinted in Appendix A.

Many of the styles you might find in a set of open source normalizing styles are most helpful when dealing with legacy browsers, so it's entirely possible that they might not be necessary for your project (depending on which browsers it supports). You might also find that styles are included for a lot of elements that you're not using, like <audio>, <canvas>, <kbd>, and more. If you have no plans to use some of the included elements you should consider removing their styles in the interest of having smaller CSS files.

Base Styles

Base styles are styles whose intent is to provide a starting point from which other, more specialized styles can be built up. They can be identified easily because they are applied to HTML elements using single type selectors or very simple combinations of type selectors and combinators (ul ul to target unordered lists within unordered lists, for example) and any pseudoclasses that apply to them. Along with normalizing styles, base styles are the least specific styles that should be found in a stylesheet.

Once a base style has been set on an HTML element it shouldn't need to be redeclared unless the style being set differs for another intended use case. The general rule of thumb to keep in mind when writing base styles is that as additional styles are applied to elements, they shouldn't need to override lots of base style declarations to accomplish design goals.

Defining Base Styles

Following are some suggestions for how to approach defining base styles for different types of commonly used elements. Many of the suggested properties are usually set by the user agent stylesheet, but they may not be set with values that are appropriate for every design, and those values might change over time as new browser versions are released. Think about the majority of use cases the elements will be styled for, and that will provide guidance for the values that should be set.

Base styles should only set properties and values for the most generic of use cases. Properties that are commonly set include:

- color
- font-family
- font-size
- font-weight
- letter-spacing
- line-height
- margin
- padding

If your website is mostly informational in nature, setting just these styles will likely get you far. However, if you are building a more application-like website with a more intricate design, setting these properties will only get you started; more complex styles might be needed for reusable components, as we'll see later in this chapter.

The properties in this list should be considered when writing your base styles, but they don't need to be set 100% of the time, as all are inherited from their ancestors (except margin and padding). If margin and padding values should be inherited, this can be accomplished by using the value inherit for each of those properties. Any additional properties or pseudoclasses that should be considered for inclusion in base styles for a particular type of element are included in the following sections.

Leveraging Inheritance

The color, font-family, font-size, font-weight, letter-spacing, and line-height properties are usually inherited from parent elements by child elements, so these values don't always need to be set. For a complete list of CSS properties and information on if their values are inherited, visit *https://www.w3.org/TR/CSS21/propidx.html*. For a complete list of HTML elements to style, visit *https://www.w3.org/TR/html-markup/elements.html*.

Document Metadata

Document metadata tags include the <head>, <title>, <base>, <link>, and <meta> tags. Since they are not visible, they cannot be styled.

Sectioning Elements

Sectioning elements include the <address>, <article>, <aside>, <body>, <footer>, <header>, <nav>, and <section> elements. These elements usually contain other elements and comprise the various sections of an HTML document.

Consider setting the following properties on sectioning elements:

- color
- font-family
- font-size
- font-weight
- letter-spacing
- line-height
- padding

Setting the background property might also be helpful for the <body> element. Example 4-2 shows how base styles can be applied to sectioning elements.

Example 4-2. Base styles for sectioning elements

```
body {
  background: #FFFFFF;
  color: #333333;
  font-family: Helvetica, Arial, sans-serif;
  font-size: 14px;
  line-height: 1.3;
  padding: 5% 20%;
}

article,
footer,
header,
nav {
  padding: 0;
}

article,
nav {
  margin-bottom: 12px;
  margin-top: 12px;
}

footer {
  margin-top: 12px;
}

header {
  margin-bottom: 12px;
}
```

Heading and Text Elements

Heading elements include the <h1>–<h6> elements and are intended to define the topic of each different section in an HTML document. Text elements include the <figure>, <figcaption>, <p>, and <pre> elements and are intended to display blocks of text.

Properties that should be considered when defining base styles for heading and text elements include:

- font-family
- font-size
- font-weight
- letter-spacing

- `line-height`

- `margin-bottom`

- `margin-top`

Example 4-3 shows how base styles can be applied to heading and text elements.

Example 4-3. Base styles for heading and text elements

```
h1,
h2,
h3,
h4,
h5,
h6 {
  font-family: Georgia, Times, serif;
  font-weight: 100;
  line-height: 1.1;
  margin: 0.5em 0;
}

h1 {
  font-size: 36px;
}

h2 {
  font-size: 24px;
}

h3 {
  font-size: 21px;
}

h4 {
  font-size: 18px;
}

h5 {
  font-size: 16px;
}

h6 {
  font-size: 14px;
}

p,
pre {
  margin-bottom: 12px;
  margin-top: 12px;
}
```

Anchor Tags

Anchor tags provide links to other HTML documents or other sections of the same HTML document. They can make use of the :link, :visited, :focus, :hover, and :active pseudoclasses that are commonly used to show state, so when defining base styles it's important to keep these pseudoclasses in mind. Here's a breakdown of what each pseudoclass is used for:

- :link styles are applied to elements that have a valid href attribute.

- :visited styles are applied to links that have a valid href attribute whose location appears in the browser's history.

- :focus styles are applied when a link element has received focus. This occurs when the element is clicked or tapped, or when the Tab key is used to navigate to the element.

- :hover styles are applied when the mouse pointer is placed over a link. On touch devices, since there is no hover state, :hover styles are usually applied when an element is tapped, and the styles are removed when a different element is tapped.

- :active styles are applied when a link is "activated." When using a mouse this happens after the link has been clicked but before the mouse button has been released. On touch devices, this occurs when an element is tapped but before the finger is released.

It's also important to ensure that if they are set, the :link and :visited pseudoclasses are the first two defined. All of these pseudoclasses have the same specificity, so the cascade will apply them based on order. This means that if a link has been visited and :visited is defined after :hover, :focus, or :active, any overlapping styles defined for the :visited pseudoclass will take precedence.

Another thing to keep in mind is that all of these pseudoclasses effectively give links a higher specificity because they are comprised of one type selector and one pseudoclass selector. This means that overriding those styles requires a higher specificity or an equal specificity that appears later in the stylesheet. For this reason, the :link pseudoclass is often ignored and the styles that would be applied are instead set directly using the a type selector.

Common properties that should be considered when defining base styles for anchor tags and their pseudoclasses include:

- background-color
- border
- color

- `font-weight`

- `text-decoration`

Although the browser's defaults usually suffice, defining the `outline-width`, `outline-style`, and `outline-color` properties (or the more concise `outline` shorthand property) can be helpful when styling the `:focus` pseudoclass.

 Removing a link's use of the `outline` property on `:focus` without replacing it with another visual cue is considered poor form as it hinders usability for those navigating with just a keyboard or another accessibility device.

Anchor tags are commonly inline by default as they are used to modify text or other inline elements. `font-family`, `font-size`, and `font-weight` could also be set, but more than likely values for these properties will be inherited. Example 4-4 shows how base styles can be applied to anchor tag elements.

Example 4-4. Base styles for links

```
a,
a:visited,
a:focus,
a:hover,
a:active {
  color: inherit;
  text-decoration: underline;
}

a:hover {
  background-color: #FFFF00;
}
```

Text Semantics

Text semantics are elements that are used to give text more meaning or structure. These elements are usually inline and include the `<abbr>`, `<b>`, `<cite>`, `<code>`, `<data>`, `<dfn>`, `<em>`, `<i>`, `<kbd>`, `<s>`, `<strong>`, `<sub>`, `<sup>`, `<time>`, and `<u>` tags, among others.

As these elements are used to modify text, the following properties should be considered when defining their base styles:

- `color`

- `font-family`

- font-size
- font-weight

For example, styles for the <code> tag might be defined as follows:

```
code {
  color: #00FF00;
  font-family: monospace;
  font-weight: 500;
  line-height: 1.5;
}
```

Lists

List elements include the <ol> (ordered list), <ul> (unordered list), and <dl> (definition list) elements. Ordered and unordered lists can only immediately contain <li> (list item) elements and definition lists can only immediately contain <dt> (definition term) and <dd> (definition description) elements.

Because of their versatility, it can be difficult to determine appropriate base styles for lists. If a website is mostly informational it is common to display lists as numbered or bulleted or as appropriately indented definitions, but if a website has a more intricate user interface, lists may be used in a number of different scenarios that require other styling to match a given design. Some of these scenarios might include horizontal navigation, a list of products for sale, details in a social media profile, and so on.

The following properties should be considered when defining base styles for ordered and unordered list elements:

- font-family
- font-size
- list-style-type or list-style-image
- list-style-position
- line-height
- margin-bottom
- margin-top
- padding-left

For a purely informational website, it might make sense to set the list-style-type or list-style-image and list-style-position properties to help enumerate the items in the list. However, for a more application-like website it might make even more sense to simply assign the value none to these properties if they will rarely be used in order to prevent having to constantly override them. To prevent child elements from being indented, padding-left should be set to 0 on the <ol> or <ul> element. Child <li> elements inherit font-family, font-size, and line-height properties from their parent <ol> or <ul> element, but not margin or padding properties.

An unordered list might be assigned the following styles:

```
ul {
  list-style-position: outside;
  list-style-type: disc;
  margin-top: 0;
  margin-bottom: 12px;
}

ul ul {
    margin-bottom: 0;
}
```

You can style the same properties for definition lists as for ordered and unordered lists, though it's not very common to use list-style-type, list-style-image, or list-style-position as those styles only apply to elements that have the display property set to list-item. list-item is the default value for the display property of li elements, but block is typically the default for <dt> and <dd> elements.

<dd> and <dt> elements inherit font-family, font-size, and line-height properties from their parent <dl> element, and it is common for <dd> elements to have margin-left set to create an indented effect (to avoid this, assign this property a value of 0).

Grouping Elements

Grouping elements include <div>, <main>, and <span>. Although the <span> tag is technically a text-level semantic, its main use is for grouping text or inline elements.

The <div> and <main> tags are typically block-level elements, whereas the <span> tag is inline. Because these elements are simply used for grouping other tags, they don't usually warrant any base styles; their styling will vary on a case-by-case basis denoted by classes. If, however, the <main> tag is used as a visual container, it might benefit from having values set for margin and padding.

Tables

As the name suggests, tables display data within a tabular structure. Elements used for displaying tabular data include the <table>, <caption>, <colgroup>, <col> (column), <tbody> (table body), <thead> (table header), <tfoot> (table footer), <tr> (table row), <td> (table cell), and <th> (table header cell) elements. In the late 1990s and early 2000s it was common to use tables to create page layouts, but now that CSS and browsers have matured it makes more sense to leave that to other styled elements and instead use tables to only display tabular data.

The following properties should be considered when defining base styles for `<table>` elements:

- `border-collapse`
- `border-spacing`
- `border` (`border-width`, `border-color`, `border-style`)
- `empty-cells`
- `font-family`
- `font-size`
- `letter-spacing`
- `line-height`

The following properties should be considered when defining base styles for `<thead>`, `<tbody>`, and `<tfoot>` elements:

- `background-color`
- `color`
- `text-align`
- `vertical-align`

And these properties should be considered when defining base styles for `<th>` and `<td>` elements:

- `background-color`
- `border` (`border-width`, `border-color`, `border-style`)
- `color`
- `font-family`
- `font-size`
- `letter-spacing`
- `line-height`
- `text-align`
- `vertical-align`

Given these considerations, base table styles might resemble something like the following:

```
table {
  border-collapse: collapse;
  border-spacing: 0;
  empty-cells: show;
  border: 1px solid #000000;
}

tfoot,
thead {
  text-align: left;
}

thead {
  background-color: #ACACAC;
  color: #000000;
}

th,
td {
  border-left: 1px solid #000000;
  padding: 0.5em 1em;
}

th:first-child,
td:first-child {
  border-left: none;
}
```

Forms

Forms are used for gathering information from users and include the <form>, <label>, <input>, <button>, <select>, <datalist>, <optgroup>, <option>, <textarea>, <output>, <progress>, <meter>, <fieldset>, and <legend> elements. As usual, properties that should be considered when declaring base styles include:

- font-family
- font-size
- line-height
- margin
- padding

Styles can be set on the <form> element and inherited by its children for basic designs, but more complicated designs may warrant more styling. It's common for <legend>, <label>, and <input> elements to have differing values set for font-weight, font-size, and font-family, in which case those values need to be set on the element.

Some form elements can be difficult to style because many browsers simply ignore properties that are applied to them. For example, attempting to apply border-color, border-width, background-color, and a number of other properties on checkboxes and radio buttons results in the browser ignoring the desired styles. This can be overcome by creating custom checkbox and radio button components that hide the form control and use other HTML elements to represent the visual metaphor, but this is not the job of base styles.

Form elements might be reasonably assigned the following styles:

```css
fieldset {
  border: 0;
  margin: 0;
  padding: 0;
}

input {
  display: block;
  font-size: inherit;
  padding: 4px;
  width: 100%;
}

label {
  display: block;
  font-weight: 900;
  margin-bottom: 6px;
  padding: 4px;
}

legend {
  border: 0;
  color: #000000;
  display: block;
  font-size: 1.2em;
  margin-bottom: 12px;
  padding: 0 12px;
  width: 100%;
}
```

Images

Graphics can be displayed using the <img> or <picture> tags. Properties that should be considered when declaring base styles include:

- border

- `max-width`

- `vertical-align`

Because `<img>` elements can be used in inline formatting contexts, `baseline` is the default value assigned to the `vertical-align` property, which may or may not be appropriate for the design being implemented. Additionally, when `<img>` elements are displayed within sized block-level elements, it's common to prevent the image from overflowing its container by assigning it a `max-width` equal to `100%` of its parent container.

Base styles for the `img` tag might be defined as follows:

```
img {
  border: none;
  max-width: 100%;
  vertical-align: middle;
}
```

Component Styles

Reusable components are elements or groups of elements that are styled to employ visual metaphors that make it easier to interact with a website. Some examples of reusable components include buttons, drop-down menus, modal windows, progress bars, and tabs.

Reusable components are easy to recognize, but they can be difficult to build correctly. Before building a reusable component it's helpful to answer the following questions:

- Will this be a standalone component or will there be more than one grouped together?

- Will this component typically behave like an inline element, a block-level element, or in some other way (i.e., will it be positioned absolutely out of the document flow)?

With the answers to these questions in mind, the process of creating reusable components can be simplified by following a few guidelines:

1. Before building a component, define the behavior that needs to be built.

2. Keep component styles granular and set reasonable defaults.

3. Override visual styles for grouped components as needed by surrounding them with a container element that has a differentiating class.

4. Delegate the assignment of dimensions to structural containers.

The following example, which explains how to build a simple tab component (Figure 4-1), explores each of these guidelincs.

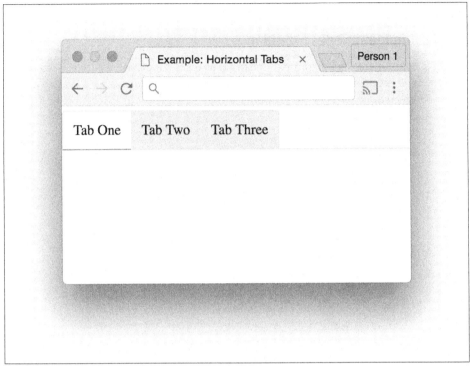

Figure 4-1. Tabs

Define the Behavior that Needs to Be Built

For this example we'll be building the tabs depicted in Figure 4-1. The requirements are as follows:

- There are three tabs in Figure 4-1, but the component should work with two or more tabs.
- When a tab is active, the bottom border turns blue and the background white.
- When a tab is inactive, the background color is gray.

We'll use the HTML in Example 4-5 to build the tabs.

Example 4-5. Markup for a group of three tabs

```
<nav>
  <ul>
    <li><a href="#">Tab One</a></li>
```

```
      <li><a href="#">Tab Two</a></li>
      <li><a href="#">Tab Three</a></li>
    </ul>
</nav>
```

Keep Component Styles Granular

Keeping component styles granular means that each should be written to style just one element, so they can be reused. In Example 4-5 there are three tabs, so a class could be created for each (as in Example 4-6), but that would just result in a lot of duplicated code.

Example 4-6. Individual classes for each tab

```
/**
 * Styling each tab individually results in lots of duplicated code.
 */
.tab-1 { /* styles go here */ }
.tab-2 { /* styles go here */ }
.tab-3 { /* styles go here */ }

.tab-1:hover { /* styles go here */ }
.tab-2:hover { /* styles go here */ }
.tab-3:hover { /* styles go here */ }

.tab-1.active { /* styles go here */ }
.tab-2.active { /* styles go here */ }
.tab-3.active { /* styles go here */ }

.tab-1 > a { /* styles go here */ }
.tab-2 > a { /* styles go here */ }
.tab-3 > a { /* styles go here */ }

.tab-group { /* styles go here */ }
```

This isn't a very good solution—each class has the same declaration block as the others, which leads to larger CSS files for clients to download and an increased risk of visual inconsistencies because there is more code to maintain. To avoid this the classes could be grouped as in Example 4-7, but there would still be a bunch of classes that do the same thing.

Example 4-7. Individual classes for a tab grouped together

```
/**
 * Grouping tabs like this results in lots of unnecessary duplicated classes.
 */

.tab-1,
.tab-2,
```

```
.tab-3 {
  /* styles go here */
}

.tab-1:hover,
.tab-2:hover,
.tab-3:hover {
  /* styles go here */
}

.tab-1.active,
.tab-2.active,
.tab-3.active {
  /* styles go here */
}

.tab-1 > a,
.tab-2 > a,
.tab-3 > a {
  /* styles go here */
}

.tab-group {
  /* styles go here */
}
```

The best solution is to abstract the styles into a reusable class (Example 4-8). Note
that there is also an .active class that can be conditionally applied to indicate which
tab is active, as well as styles for a .tab-group element that contains multiple tabs.

Example 4-8. Styles for a tab

```
/**
 * Tab Component Styles
 */

.tab {
  background-color: #F2F2F2;
  border-bottom: 1px solid #EEEEEE;
  border-top: 1px solid #EEEEEE;
  bottom: -1px;
  display: inline-block;
  margin-left: 0;
  margin-right: 0;
  margin-top: 4px;
  position: relative;
}

.tab:first-child {
  border-left: 1px solid #EEEEEE;
  border-top-left-radius: 4px;
```

```css
}

.tab:last-child {
  border-right: 1px solid #EEEEEE;
  border-top-right-radius: 4px;
}

.tab.active {
  background-color: #FFFFFF;
  border-bottom: 1px solid #2196F3;
  color: #000000;
}

.tab:hover {
  background-color: #F9F9F9;
}

.tab > a {
  color: inherit;
  display: block;
  height: 100%;
  padding: 12px;
  text-decoration: none;
  width: 100%;
}

/**
 * Tab Component Containers
 */

.tab-group {
  border-bottom: 1px solid #EEEEEE;
  list-style: none;
  margin: 0;
  padding-left: 0;
}
```

Now that we have these styles assigned to the appropriate classes we can update the HTML to make use of them, as in Example 4-9.

Example 4-9. Markup for a group of three tabs with new tab class

```html
<nav>
  <ul class="tab-group">
    <li class="tab active"><a href="#">Tab One</a></li>
    <li class="tab"><a href="#">Tab Two</a></li>
    <li class="tab"><a href="#">Tab Three</a></li>
  </ul>
</nav>
```

Let the Component's Container Override Visual Styles as Needed

At this point we have a horizontal tab component, but what if we need to also be able to display tabs vertically? When we need to use the tabs in a context in which they are styled differently, we'll delegate the responsibility of defining those styles to the parent container. To accomplish this, we'll create a new `.tab-group-vertical` class that will also contain `.tab` elements and group it with the `.tab-group` class:

```
.tab-group,
.tab-group-vertical {
  list-style: none;
  margin: 0;
  padding-left: 0;
}
```

Next, we'll move some of the declarations made in the `.tab` ruleset to rulesets with more specific selectors so new classes don't have to always override them. The `.tab` class will now only contain styles that are applicable to all tabs:

```
.tab {
  background-color: #F2F2F2;
  margin-left: 0;
  margin-right: 0;
  position: relative;
}

.tab:hover {
  background-color: #F9F9F9;
}

.tab.active {
  background-color: #FFFFFF;
  color: #000000;
}
```

The `border`, `border-radius`, and `display` styles should now be delegated to appropriately scoped selectors, and the `.tab-group` and `.tab-group-vertical` classes should each receive their own differing border styles (Example 4-10).

Example 4-10. Delegating properties to appropriate containers

```
/**
 * Horizontal Tab Groups
 */

.tab-group {
  border-bottom: 1px solid #EEEEEE;
}

.tab-group .tab {
```

```
  border-bottom: 1px solid #EEEEEE;
  border-top: 1px solid #EEEEEE;
  bottom: -1px;
  display: inline-block;
}

.tab-group .tab:first-child {
  border-left: 1px solid #EEEEEE;
  border-top-left-radius: 4px;
}

.tab-group .tab:last-child {
  border-right: 1px solid #EEEEEE;
  border-top-right-radius: 4px;
}

.tab-group .tab.active {
  border-bottom: 1px solid #2196F3;
}


/**
 * Vertical Tab Groups
 */

.tab-group-vertical {
  border-left: 1px solid #EEEEEE;
}

.tab-group-vertical .tab {
  border-left: 1px solid #EEEEEE;
  border-right: 1px solid #EEEEEE;
  left: -1px;
  display: block;
}

.tab-group-vertical .tab:first-child {
  border-top: 1px solid #EEEEEE;
  border-top-right-radius: 4px;
}

.tab-group-vertical .tab:last-child {
  border-bottom: 1px solid #EEEEEE;
  border-bottom-right-radius: 4px;
}

.tab-group-vertical .tab.active {
  border-left: 1px solid #2196F3;
}
```

One last thing you may have noticed is that 1px solid #EEEEEE appears over and
over. We can refactor this by setting the border-color and border-style properties

on the `.tab` class and then appropriately setting the `border-width` and overriding the `border-color` property when necessary, like in Example 4-11. This is advantageous because in the event that this color needs to be changed, there will be fewer places that need to be updated.

Example 4-11. Markup for a group of three tabs with new tab class

```
/**
 * Tab Component Styles
 */

.tab {
  background-color: #F2F2F2;
  margin-left: 0;
  margin-right: 0;
  position: relative;
}

.tab:hover {
  background-color: #F9F9F9;
}

.tab.active {
  background-color: #FFFFFF;
  color: #000000;
}

.tab > a {
  color: inherit;
  display: block;
  height: 100%;
  padding: 12px;
  text-decoration: none;
  width: 100%;
}

/**
 * Tab Component Containers
 */

.tab-group,
.tab-group-vertical {
  list-style: none;
  margin: 0;
  padding-left: 0;
}

.tab,
.tab-group,
.tab-group-vertical {
  border-color: #EEEEEE;
```

```
    border-style: solid;
    border-width: 0;
}

/**
 * Horizontal Tab Groups
 */

.tab-group {
    border-bottom-width: 1px;
}

.tab-group .tab {
    border-bottom-width: 1px;
    border-top-width: 1px;
    bottom: -1px;
    display: inline-block;
}

.tab-group .tab:first-child {
    border-left-width: 1px;
    border-top-left-radius: 4px;
}

.tab-group .tab:last-child {
    border-right-width: 1px;
    border-top-right-radius: 4px;
}

.tab-group .tab.active {
    border-bottom-color: #2196F3;
    border-bottom-width: 1px;
}


/**
 * Vertical Tab Groups
 */

.tab-group-vertical {
    border-left-width: 1px;
}

.tab-group-vertical .tab {
    border-left-width: 1px;
    border-right-width: 1px;
    left: -1px;
    display: block;
}

.tab-group-vertical .tab:first-child {
    border-top-width: 1px;
```

```
    border-top-right-radius: 4px;
}

.tab-group-vertical .tab:last-child {
  border-bottom-width: 1px;
  border-bottom-right-radius: 4px;
}

.tab-group-vertical .tab.active {
  border-left-color: #2196F3;
  border-left-width: 1px;
}
```

When a group of tabs present in a .tab-group-vertical element are rendered using the CSS in Example 4-11 you'll see the tabs in Figure 4-2.

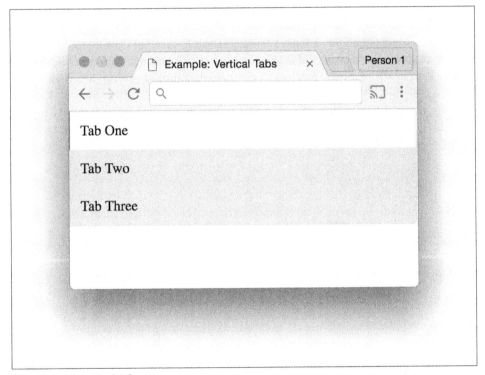

Figure 4-2. Vertical tabs

These tabs aren't quite right yet, but we'll take care of that next by delegating the assignment of dimensions to the component's structural container.

Delegate the Assignment of Dimensions to Structural Containers

You may have noticed that in the CSS we wrote for the `.tab-group` and `.tab-group-vertical` components' dimensions weren't specified. This omission was intentional, because the responsibility for assigning dimensions should be delegated to the structure that contains the component or component group. *Structural styles*, described in the next section, are styles that dictate the basic structure of a page. There are any number of different layouts you can build, including those with sidebars, columns, or whatever you dream up.

Components are intended to be reusable, so it's difficult to predict all of the different places where they'll appear. This is why it's important to delegate the responsibility of setting dimensions to the elements that are actually housing the components.

For example, let's assume that we want to display two horizontal groups of tabs that each occupy 50% of the available visible area for desktop browsers, as shown in Figure 4-3. We could add a `width: 50%` declaration to the `.tab-group` definition, but that wouldn't be very reusable if we needed to use the tabs at a different width elsewhere. Instead, Example 4-12 delegates the responsibility of setting dimensions to a structural element that has the `.tabbed-pane` class. You probably wouldn't want to use this many different sets of tabs on the same page, but the example is merely intended as an illustration of how to delegate the responsibility of setting dimensions.

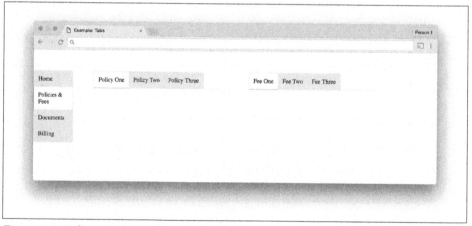

Figure 4-3. Delegating component dimensions to a structural container

Example 4-12. Code that delegates component dimensions to a structural container

```
<!doctype html>
<html>
  <head>
    <title>Example: Tabs</title>
    <style type="text/css">
```

```css
*,
*:after,
*:before {
  box-sizing: border-box;
}

body {
  margin: 0;
  padding: 0;
}

/**
 * Tab Component Styles
 */

.tab {
  background-color: #F2F2F2;
  margin-left: 0;
  margin-right: 0;
  position: relative;
}

.tab:hover {
  background-color: #F9F9F9;
}

.tab.active {
  background-color: #FFFFFF;
  color: #000000;
}

.tab > a {
  color: inherit;
  display: block;
  height: 100%;
  padding: 12px;
  text-decoration: none;
  width: 100%;
}

/**
 * Tab Component Containers
 */

.tab-group,
.tab-group-vertical {
  list-style: none;
  margin: 0;
  padding-left: 0;
}

  .tab,
```

```
.tab-group,
.tab-group-vertical {
  border-color: #EEEEEE;
  border-style: solid;
  border-width: 0;
}

/**
 * Horizontal Tab Groups
 */

.tab-group {
  border-bottom-width: 1px;
}

.tab-group .tab {
  border-bottom-width: 1px;
  border-top-width: 1px;
  bottom: -1px;
  display: inline-block;
}

.tab-group .tab:first-child {
  border-left-width: 1px;
  border-top-left-radius: 4px;
}

.tab-group .tab:last-child {
  border-right-width: 1px;
  border-top-right-radius: 4px;
}

.tab-group .tab.active {
  border-bottom-color: #2196F3;
  border-bottom-width: 1px;
}


/**
 * Vertical Tab Groups
 */

.tab-group-vertical {
  border-left-width: 1px;
}

.tab-group-vertical .tab {
  border-left-width: 1px;
  border-right-width: 1px;
  left: -1px;
  display: block;
}
```

```css
.tab-group-vertical .tab:first-child {
  border-top-width: 1px;
  border-top-right-radius: 4px;
}

.tab-group-vertical .tab:last-child {
  border-bottom-width: 1px;
  border-bottom-right-radius: 4px;
}

.tab-group-vertical .tab.active {
  border-left-color: #2196F3;
  border-left-width: 1px;
}

/**
 * Tab Component Containers
 */

.tabbed-pane {
  display: block;
  width: 100%;
}

.tabbed-pane .tab-group {
  float: left;
  width: 45%;
}

.tabbed-pane .tab-group:first-child {
  margin-right: 5%;
}

.tabbed-pane .tab-group:last-child {
  margin-left: 5%;
}

/**
 * Structural Styles
 */

.global-nav {
  float: left;
  padding: 5% 0;
  width: 10%
}

.content {
  float: left;
  padding: 5%;
  width: 80%;
```

```
      }
    </style>
  </head>
  <body>
    <nav class="global-nav">
      <ul class="tab-group-vertical">
        <li class="tab"><a href="#">Home</a>
        <li class="tab active"><a href="#">Policies &amp; Fees</a>
        <li class="tab"><a href="#">Documents</a>
        <li class="tab"><a href="#">Billing</a>
      </ul>
    </nav>

    <main class="content">
      <nav class="tabbed-pane">
        <ul class="tab-group">
          <li class="tab active"><a href="#">Policy One</a>
          <li class="tab"><a href="#">Policy Two</a>
          <li class="tab"><a href="#">Policy Three</a>
        </ul>
        <ul class="tab-group">
          <li class="tab active"><a href="#">Fee One</a>
          <li class="tab"><a href="#">Fee Two</a>
          <li class="tab"><a href="#">Fee Three</a>
        </ul>
      </nav>
    </main>
  </body>
</html>
```

Structural Styles

Structural styles contain components and their containers, just like the .tabbed-pane element in Example 4-12. Since layouts need dimensions, it's easy to delegate setting the dimensions to structural styles and then simply add in components and their containers. Example 4-13 is code for a simple layout that contains a header, sidebar, and content area (Figure 4-4). When the viewport gets too small, the header, sidebar, and content area stack vertically (Figure 4-5).

Example 4-13. Layout with a header, sidebar, and content area

```
<!doctype html>
<html>
  <head>
    <title>Layout Example</title>
    <style type="text/css">
    *,
    *:after,
    *:before {
```

```
    box-sizing: border-box;
  }

  html,
  body,
  main  {
    height: 100%;
    margin: 0;
    width: 100%;
  }

  .layout-header {
    background-color: #DDDD88;
    display: block;
    min-height: 10%;
    width: 100%;
  }

  .layout-header,
  .layout-sidebar,
  .layout-content {
    text-align: center;
  }

  .layout-sidebar,
  .layout-content {
    float: left;
    height: 100%;
  }

  .layout-sidebar {
    background-color: #8888BB;
    width: 20%;
  }
  .layout-content {
    background-color: #EEBB55;
    width: 80%;
  }

  @media all and (max-width: 640px) {
    .layout-header,
    .layout-sidebar,
    .layout-content {
      display: block;
      float: none;
      height: auto;
      min-height: 100px;
      width: 100%;
    }
  }
  </style>
</head>
```

```
<body>
  <main>
    <header class="layout-header">Header</header>
    <div class="layout-sidebar">Sidebar</div>
    <div class="layout-content">Content</div>
  </main>
</body>
</html>
```

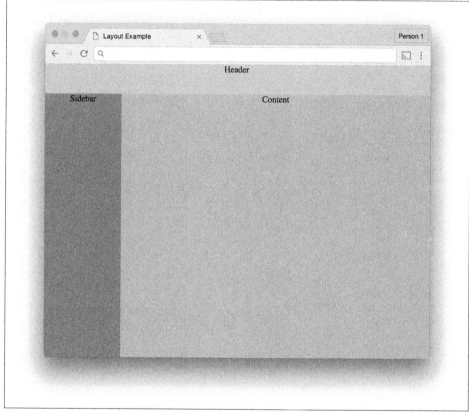

Figure 4-4. Layout with a header, sidebar, and content area

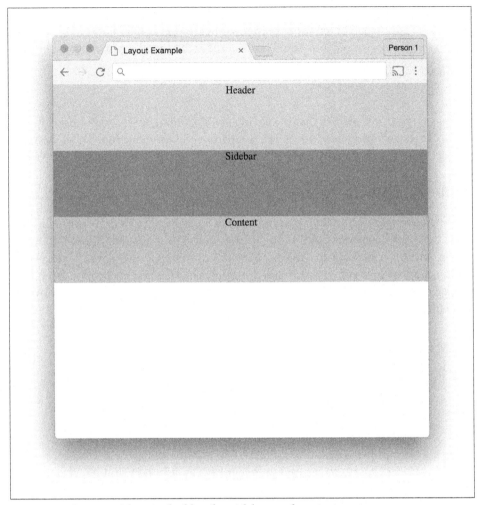

Figure 4-5. Layout with a stacked header, sidebar, and content area

Utility Styles

We learned in Chapter 2 that the !important declaration overrides the cascade by telling the browser that a declaration should be used for elements that match its containing ruleset's selectors regardless of the specificity of the declaration block's selector. Misuse of !important leads to confusing CSS: if it's used in multiple declaration blocks to style the same element, the order in which those rulesets appear will determine which styles get applied.

One way to avoid confusion is to avoid using !important entirely, but used sparingly it can be very helpful. *Utility styles* are styles that get applied to elements either by a prudent developer when she is defining the classes that appear on an HTML element, or by JavaScript when a certain condition is met. For example, if pressing a button hides a particular element, this could be achieved by adding the following class:

```
.hidden {
  display: none !important;
}
```

Adding `!important` ensures that the element will continue to be hidden regardless of other classes that are added to or removed from the element, (unless, of course, a conflicting `display` property augmented by `!important` is added after).

Browser-Specific Styles

Older browsers have quirks that can often be overcome by using *browser-specific CSS hacks* that trick the browser into acting the way you expect it to. For example, due to a bug in Internet Explorer 7 the `inline-block` value does not always work as expected for the `display` property, but it is still possible to make elements behave like inline-block elements. To do this you'll have to trick the browser by using the CSS shown in Example 4-14.

Example 4-14. The inline-block hack for IE7

```
.selector {
  display: inline-block;
  *display: inline;
  zoom: 1;
}
```

There are two problems with this code: the `*display` property is not valid because it's a syntax error (property names cannot begin with an asterisk), and you're cluttering up your CSS with a hack for an obsolete browser. If you absolutely cannot drop support for an old browser that needs hacks like this, you should keep these hacks separate and be sure to leave behind comments explaining what the code does. For example, if you need to use a CSS hack for older versions of Internet Explorer, you could keep these hacks in their own stylesheet and add them to the page using conditional comments that only load those styles for a particular version of the browser:

```
<!--[if IE 7]>
  <link rel="stylesheet" href="ie7.css" type="text/css" />
<![endif]-->
```

Chapter Summary

This chapter described the various intents that styles can have. Although the ideas in this chapter are fairly simple, they can be very powerful; as we'll see in Chapter 6, a solid understanding of the different intents as well as the functionality of the cascade makes organizing and reusing CSS much easier. Before we get to that, though, we'll talk about testing.

Testing

Testing CSS can be difficult because there are so many different platforms, screen sizes, and form factors that need to be tested. This chapter explores how to determine which browsers and devices need to be tested as well as a number of different ways to test and maintain your CSS. By the end of this chapter you should have a better idea of how to approach testing your CSS, which will result in a higher level of confidence when making changes.

Why Is Testing Difficult?

Thoroughly testing CSS changes can take a long time and requires a lot of different tools.

There are many factors to consider, including:

- Which browser is the page being tested on?
- How do you test various browsers on different operating systems?
- What size is the window that the page is being viewed in?
- How can a large number of pages be tested quickly?
- How do you verify that what you're seeing is correct?
- How can a website be tested on other devices if you don't have access to those specific devices?

Which Browsers Are Important to Test?

Before testing, it's important to know which browsers should be tested. Ideally you will only need to support browsers that are being used to view your website by a minimum number of people (the particular threshold can vary from company to company). You can identify these fairly easily by using an analytics tool that breaks down all of the browsers and devices and the versions of each that are used by the website's visitors.

Browser Market Share

It's important to support all of the major browsers that have been released in the past couple of years. Recent versions of Chrome, Firefox, Safari, Microsoft Edge (formerly Internet Explorer), and their mobile counterparts have done a great job of being standards-compliant, so there is less fragmentation in browser behavior than there once was. Each of these browsers offers automatic updates too, which means that as time goes on more people will have up-to-date modern browsers.

Unfortunately, though, some people still use old browsers. For example, at the time of writing the top three most used versions of Microsoft Edge/Internet Explorer according to NetMarketShare were Internet Explorer 11, Internet Explorer 8, and Edge 13, in that order (Figure 5-1).

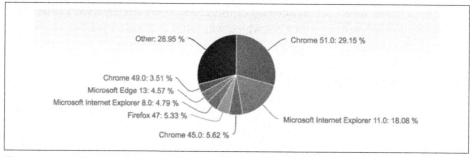

Figure 5-1. Desktop browser market share in July 2016, according to NetMarketShare

If your website isn't being frequented by people using old browsers, then you probably don't have to worry about maintaining your code for them. However, if older browsers account for a sizeable percentage of your traffic, then you might want to consider supporting them, especially if your website is generating revenue.

Accessing Browser Statistics and Screen Resolutions in Google Analytics

Google Analytics (*http://www.google.com/analytics*) is a freemium service offered by Google and is one of the most commonly used analytics packages; it tracks website traffic, user behavior, and much more. Let's look at two pieces of information that are important to refactoring CSS: browser information and screen resolutions.

Finding Browser Statistics and Screen Resolutions in Other Analytics Tools

If you're using something other than Google Analytics you might still be able to get data about the browsers and screen resolutions being used to view your website. Please refer to your analytics tool's documentation for more information.

Browser information

At the time of writing, browser information can be found in Google Analytics in the Audience → Technology → Browser & OS menu when "Browser" is selected as the primary dimension (Figure 5-2). Once there, clicking on a browser will reveal the statistics for each version of that browser that has visited your website, as seen in Figure 5-3. This information will provide the necessary information to determine which browsers are being used to view your website. If you find that you're spending a considerable amount of time writing CSS to support an old browser that very few people are actually using to view your site, you should consider dropping support for that browser.

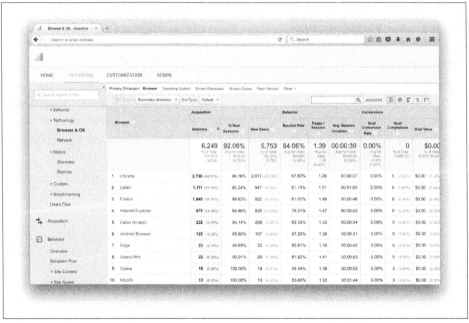

Figure 5-2. The Browser & OS screen in Google Analytics

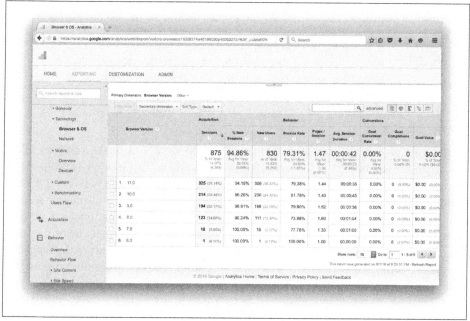

Figure 5-3. The breakdown of browser versions in Google Analytics

Screen resolutions

Information on screen resolutions can also be found in Google Analytics in the Audience → Technology → Browser & OS menu, when "Screen Resolution" is selected as the primary dimension (Figure 5-4). This data indicates the screen sizes at which your website is being viewed and can be helpful in determining the most common use cases that should be designed for.

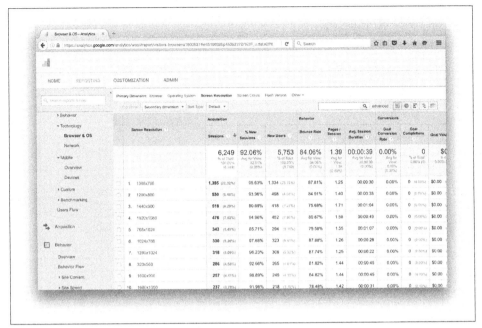

Figure 5-4. Screen resolutions in Google Analytics

Testing with Multiple Browsers

The most common way to test CSS across browsers is to do so manually. You'll prob-ably want to download all of the major mainstream browsers:

- Google Chrome (*http://www.google.com/chrome*)
- Firefox (*https://www.mozilla.org/firefox*)
- Safari (*https://www.apple.com/safari*)
- Microsoft Edge (*https://www.microsoft.com/en-us/windows/microsoft-edge*)

For mobile testing, you'll need to download browsers from the appropriate market-place for your device.

Safari for iOS

Safari for iOS can be tested using the native application on an iOS device or the iOS Simulator for Xcode. You can download Xcode for free from the Apple App Store (Figure 5-5), but unfortunately Xcode only runs on Mac OS; it cannot be installed on Windows.

Figure 5-5. Xcode in the App Store

Once you've installed Xcode, you can open the iOS Simulator by navigating to Xcode → Open Developer Tool → iOS Simulator. Once the iOS Simulator is running, you can launch Safari and view websites (Figure 5-6).

Figure 5-6. Emulating Safari in iOS Simulator

Android

Android devices can be tested in emulators using Android Studio (Figure 5-7), which you can download for free at *http://developer.android.com*.

Figure 5-7. The Android Studio landing page

Once you've installed Android Studio, you can create and launch emulators by creating an empty project and then selecting an emulator from the Tools → Android → AVD Manager menu (Figure 5-8).

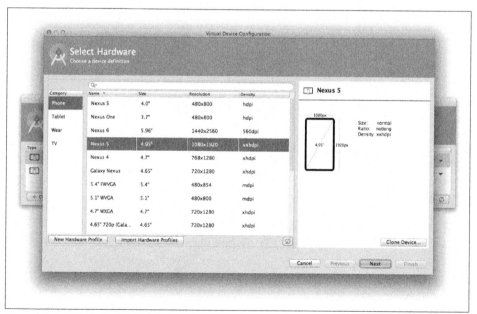

Figure 5-8. The Android Virtual Device Manager

Once you've launched an emulator you can launch a web browser from within the simulated device, much like in iOS Simulator, and use it to view websites (Figure 5-9).

Figure 5-9. Emulating an Android device

Testing with Old Versions of Browsers

Earlier in this chapter we learned how to use analytics packages to determine if your website is being frequented by people using out-of-date browsers. In some instances, you might be able to drop support for these browsers—but if you can't, you'll need to ensure that your browser works well for this demographic. The following sections contain information on how to test your website on older browsers.

Internet Explorer and Microsoft Edge

You can download Microsoft Edge and old versions of Internet Explorer for testing purposes at *https://www.modern.ie*. These browsers come as virtual machines that can be run on VirtualBox (*https://www.virtualbox.org/*), VMWare (*http://www.vmware.com/*), or Parallels (*http://www.parallels.com/*). A *virtual machine* is a piece of software that emulates an operating system, and Virtual Box, VMWare, and Parallels are programs that can run virtual machines. Virtual machines are especially helpful because programs like Internet Explorer that were compiled to run specifically on one operating system will not run on another.

Firefox

You can download old versions of Firefox at *https://support.mozilla.org/en-US/kb/install-older-version-of-firefox*. Testing an old version of Firefox is as simple as finding the version you need to test, downloading it for your operating system, and then viewing the website in that browser. If you're not developing on Windows but you are making use of the Internet Explorer virtual machines, you can also download older versions of Firefox for Windows within the virtual machine to test on that platform.

Safari and Safari for iOS

Testing old versions of Safari unfortunately requires having access to an older version of Mac OS, because Safari uses the WebKit framework found in OS X to render web pages. However, testing old versions of Safari for iOS can be done using the Xcode simulator by choosing the Hardware → Device → Manage Devices menu option and creating a new simulator with the desired operating system in the Devices window (Figure 5-10).

For more information about the iOS Simulator, see the Simulator User Guide (*http://apple.co/2fgPFNv*).

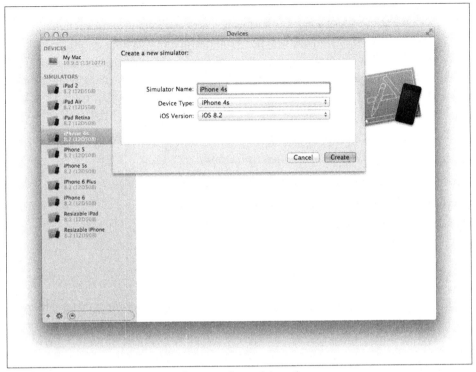

Figure 5-10. Creating a new simulator in the iOS Simulator

Chrome

Unfortunately Google doesn't provide old versions of Chrome for testing, but a new version of Chrome is released every six weeks and each new version has a very high adoption rate.

Testing the Bleeding Edge

If you're interested in seeing what's coming in the next version of Chrome, Firefox, or Safari, you can keep abreast of changes with their nightly releases:

- Chrome Canary (*https://www.google.com/chrome/browser/canary.html*)
- Firefox Aurora (*https://nightly.mozilla.org*)
- WebKit Nightly (*http://nightly.webkit.org*)

Microsoft does not provide nightly releases for Edge, but it does provide frequent early releases to members of the Windows Insider Program (*https://insider.windows.com*).

Third-Party Testing Services

An alternative to testing your website by maintaining multiple operating systems with lots of browsers and emulators is to use a third-party service. Many services are available that will allow you to test a website on any browser or form factor while providing features like sharing test sessions, manual testing on various browsers, taking screenshots, and more. Here's a selection, some of which offer a free trial or have a free tier:

- BrowserStack (*https://www.browserstack.com*)
- Sauce Labs (*https://saucelabs.com*)
- Browserling (*https://www.browserling.com*)
- Litmus (*https://litmus.com*)

Testing with Developer Tools

Each of the major browsers comes with its own set of developer tools that are there to help developers make their websites better: a number of tools are provided with each suite, each of which accomplishes a different task, but in this section only those that are relevant to testing CSS during development will be discussed.

- Chrome DevTools (*https://developer.chrome.com/devtools*)
- Safari for Developers (*https://developer.apple.com/safari/tools/*)
- Firefox Developer Tools (*https://developer.mozilla.org/en-US/docs/Tools*)
- Microsoft Edge Developer Tools (*https://dev.modern.ie/platform/documentation/f12-devtools-guide/*)

Ever-Changing Dev Tools

The instructions given here are accurate at the time of writing, but browser dev tools are constantly changing. If you find that the inevitable changes render any of the following information obsolete, please refer to the websites referenced in the preceding list for more information.

Emulating Device Sizes

Testing multiple form factors (i.e., phones, tablets, etc.) can be done by buying lots of devices, but that can get expensive quickly. Another option is to use browser developer tools to emulate the desired device dimensions. Device size can be emulated by resizing the browser window, but it's quicker to use preset dimensions. Google Chrome comes with a number of predefined dimensions that are available in the DevTools Device Mode menu.

You can access the Device Mode menu by:

- Right-clicking anywhere on the page
- Selecting "Inspect Element" to open Chrome DevTools
- Clicking the Toggle Device Mode icon (Figure 5-11)

Figure 5-11. Chrome's Toggle Device Mode icon

When you're in Device Mode, a toolbar appears at the top of the window that provides preset device dimensions and the ability to set your own (see Figure 5-12).

Figure 5-12. Device emulation in Chrome DevTools

Device size can be emulated in Firefox by entering Responsive Design mode from the Tools → Web Developer menu (Figure 5-13).

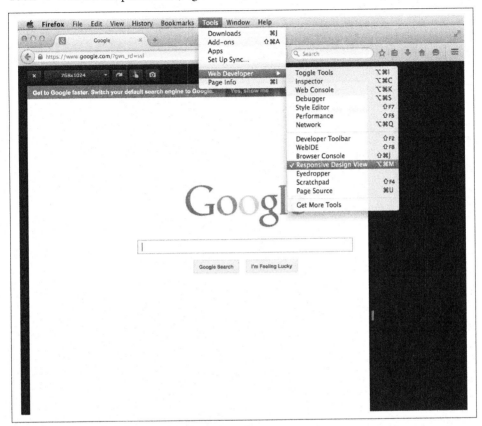

Figure 5-13. Firefox's Responsive Design mode

Safari also has a Responsive Design mode for emulating device size (Figure 5-14), accessed via the Develop → Enter Responsive Design Mode menu item.

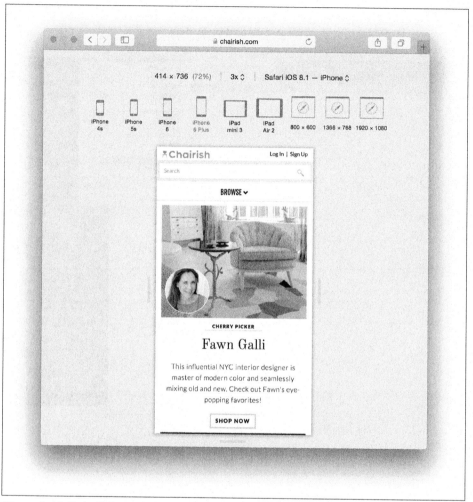

Figure 5-14. Safari's Responsive Design mode

To emulate device size in Microsoft Edge:

1. Open the F12 Developer Tools.

2. Navigate to the Emulation tab (Figure 5-15).

3. Choose a device size from the "Resolution" dropdown.

Figure 5-15. Internet Explorer's F12 Developer Tools Emulation tab

User Agent Spoofing

A *user agent* is a string that the web browser sends the server to identify itself. The developer tools found in all major browsers allow you to change the user agent, and people often assume that changing this value is effectively the same as simulating a different browser. However, user agent spoofing only changes the way the browser identifies itself; changing the user agent string does not change the browser's rendering agent.

The Document Object Model (DOM) and CSS Styles

Modern developer tools provide access to the DOM in an interactive state. Elements can be inspected or manipulated by adding, removing, or changing attributes or styles. When an element is selected from the DOM its styles can be analyzed as they are applied or as they are computed.

Figure 5-16 shows each of the CSS rules that are used to style the <body> element in a website as they are applied from various sources. Rules that are inherited are clearly labeled with the files and line numbers they originated from. Styles that are applied to the pseudo ::before and ::after elements are also clearly labeled. Rules that are crossed out are rules that have been overridden by other rules as determined by the cascade. Styles can be added or manipulated in various ways depending on which browser is being used.

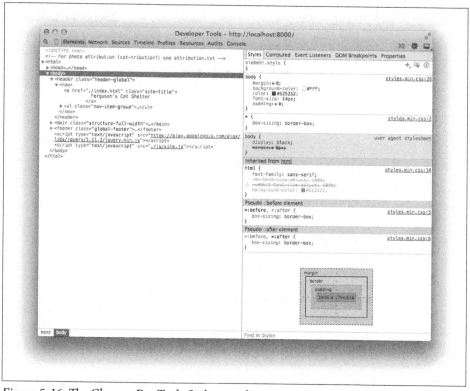

Figure 5-16. The Chrome DevTools Styles panel

Element styles can also be viewed as they would appear after being manipulated by the cascade, as can be seen in Figure 5-17. Expanding a style shows the origin file and line number of the applied style.

To view an element in the DOM, right-click it (Ctrl-click on Mac OS X), and select the "Inspect Element" option from the context menu. This will automatically open the browser's developer tools and highlight the element in the DOM explorer. The Styles panel appears next to the DOM explorer by default in Chrome, Firefox, and Edge. In Safari, you may need to click the Styles tab at the top right of the developer tools menu to view this tool.

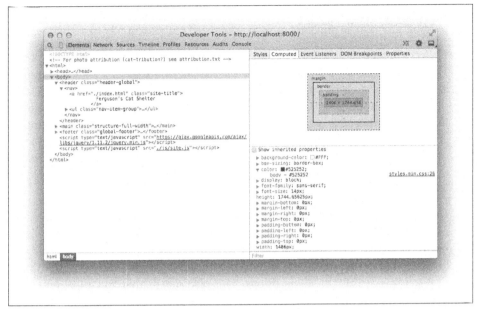

Figure 5-17. The Chrome DevTools Computed Styles tab

Visual Regression Testing

Visual regression testing is a method of testing in which a baseline image of a user interface is compared with other images of the same user interface over time to detect unintended changes (regressions). Visual regressions can be very time-consuming to test because there are lots of browsers that need to be tested, and doing this every time a change is made can result in a *lot* of testing. Additionally, it can be difficult for the naked eye to determine if small changes in spacing have occurred.

Visual regression testing can be very helpful, but like any method of testing it's not a silver bullet that will solve all of your problems. By its very nature visual regression testing is used for identifying things that have already gone wrong, so it's important to do before pushing CSS changes to production.

Tips for Visual Regression Testing

Here are some tips for visual regression testing:

Test important things
> Like with unit testing, it can be tempting to try to test every single piece of code you've written when writing visual regression tests. However, the more tests you have the more you'll have to maintain, and on top of that lots of tests aren't necessarily high-quality tests. Rather than striving for a large quantity of tests, it's important to test things that really matter. For example, once your base styles are

defined, it probably isn't very likely that they'll regress; it's more important to test reusable components that are more complicated and potentially more brittle.

Make tests granular

Visual regression testing makes it easy to test a lot of things all at once by taking a screenshot of an entire page, but it's important to avoid doing this. When a large number of components are tested together it can be difficult to determine what the actual cause of a regression is because there are so many different things going on. Instead, it's important to make your tests more granular by testing individual components one at a time. This way if there is a regression, it'll be much easier to determine the cause.

Use a variety of browsers

Using a variety of browsers for visual regression testing is extremely important since there can be inconsistencies between them. That being said, it's important not to compare screenshots across browsers because it's not productive. If one browser renders text a bit differently than another, it's probably not that big a deal unless it's really breaking things. This also means that you'll likely need to have multiple test environments available if you need to test multiple versions of Internet Explorer or Safari, as we learned earlier in this chapter.

Visual Regression Testing with Gemini

Gemini (*https://github.com/gemini-testing/gemini*) is a project developed by the Yandex team (*https://www.yandex.com*) that facilitates visual regression testing. It allows you to write a script that automates taking screenshots of elements with any major browser and then compares them against baseline images with the differences highlighted.

In this example we'll learn how to use Gemini to test an interface using the WebKit rendering engine, which is accessed through the headless browser PhantomJS (*http://phantomjs.org*). A *headless browser* is a web browser that doesn't have a user interface and is used to provide content to other programs. In addition to being able to render and screenshot websites without displaying them, headless browsers usually provide interfaces for developers to supply the browsers with instructions.

Installing Gemini

Gemini requires Node.js and NPM to be installed. You can download Node.js from *https://nodejs.org*. Installation instructions for Gemini can be found at *https://github.com/gemini-testing/gemini*. For this example Gemini will also require PhantomJS to be installed. You can download a PhantomJS binary for your operating system from *http://phantomjs.org*.

Gemini can also test other browsers using Selenium or a cloud service like Sauce Labs or BrowserStack. For detailed instructions, consult the documentation.

Configuration

Once you've installed Gemini, you need to create a file named *.gemini.js* in the root directory of your project. For this simple example, the options that need to be set are shown in Example 5-1. For a complete list of configuration options, visit *https://github.com/gemini-testing/gemini*.

Example 5-1. Gemini configuration file

```
module.exports = {
    rootUrl: 'http://127.0.0.1:8000',
    browsers: {
        phantomjs: {
            desiredCapabilities: {
                browserName: 'phantomjs'
            }
        }
    }
};
```

The code in Example 5-1 tells Gemini that the root URL is *http://127.0.0.1:8000*. Given this, as we'll see in the next section, when we write tests we'll be able to specify the URLs to test relative to this root URL. This code also tells Gemini that we will be testing with PhantomJS and that when screenshots are taken with this browser, they should use *phantomjs* as the filename. When using multiple browsers, this helps distinguish which browser took which screenshot.

Tests

Next, you need to write a test file. Gemini has its own set of functions that allow you to open a URL, select particular elements, manipulate the window, and capture a screenshot, among other things. Again, this functionality can be explored in depth in the documentation. For our example, though, we'll use the code in Example 5-2.

Example 5-2. Gemini test suite file

```
gemini.suite('animals', function(suite) {
    suite.setUrl('/')
        .setCaptureElements('.animal')
        .capture('plain')
});
```

This code (Example 5-2) is fairly straightforward. First, a test suite is declared and given a name ("animals" in this case) and a function to execute that contains tests. Then the index page of the website (/) is specified as the URL to open using setUrl. Next, the element being tested is selected with .setCaptureElements. Finally, the screenshot is captured using .capture.

Gathering baseline images

Before anything can be tested, baseline images need to be gathered so Gemini has something to compare new screenshots to. To capture baseline images, PhantomJS and Gemini first need to be run in a terminal.

Open a terminal window and issue the command phantomjs --webdriver=4444. The argument --webdriver=4444 runs PhantomJS in WebDriver mode on port 4444. This is what Gemini uses to interact with the browser.

In another terminal window, in the same directory as the *.gemini.js* file, execute the command gemini update tests/gemini/animal-tests.js to gather the baseline screenshots (*animal-tests.js* is the test file we just wrote, which is located in the *tests/gemini* directory). After the baseline images have been gathered, they are stored in a new directory, *gemini/screens/animals/plain*, in the file *phantomjs.png*. For our example we'll have just one baseline image, shown in Figure 5-18.

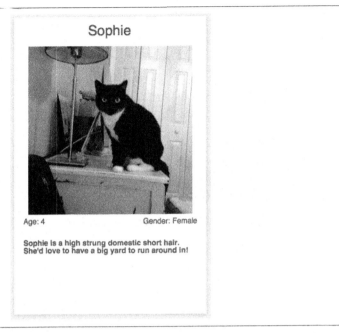

Figure 5-18. Baseline image

Testing regressions

Now that the baseline image has been gathered, we can test for regressions. Since the code we're testing is brand new and error free, we'll simply alter the code for illustrative purposes. After altering the CSS for the component being tested, run Gemini using the command `gemini test --reporter html tests/gemini/animal-tests.js`. This command instructs Gemini to run the tests, compare the screenshots, and output the results to an HTML page that is stored as *gemini-report/index.html*. Opening that file displays the test results (Figure 5-19).

Figure 5-19. Gemini report

The report generated by Gemini provides a summary of the tests and displays the screenshots it used while testing. In Figure 5-19 the difference between the two images seems to be quite large, but analyzing the baseline and current images reveals that the regression is actually a change in font size, which has the side effect of altering the dimensions of the component.

Alternatives to Gemini

There are a number of alternatives to Gemini that can be used for testing visual regressions, but two of the most popular are Wraith and PhantomCSS. Conceptually they are very similar in that they can be used to open a website, screenshot elements using either PhantomJS (a WebKit-based headless browser) or SlimerJS (a Gecko-based headless browser), and present the differences between the present and baseline versions of elements.

Wraith (*http://bbc-news.github.io/wraith/index.html*) was developed by the BBC. It depends on CasperJS, PhantomJS, or SlimerJS in addition to ImageMagick and Ruby.

PhantomCSS (*https://github.com/Huddle/PhantomCSS*) was written by James Cryer and the development team at Huddle (*http://huddle.com*). It depends on CasperJS and Resemble.JS, and can be used with PhantomJS or SlimerJS.

Maintaining Your Code

Testing code is as important as writing it, and over time maintaining quality will be just as important as new code is written. As we'll see in the next sections, code quality can be maintained by making use of coding standards and pattern libraries.

Coding Standards

Coding standards are guidelines that are written to encourage everyone on a team to write code the same way. Coding standards should be written collaboratively and reviewed and updated on a regular basis. As technology changes, coding standards can help your team keep track of the most up-to-date techniques, especially during code reviews. CSS coding standards commonly dictate conventions regarding commenting, formatting, naming, and selector usage, but they can be as specific or generic as you want.

Take a look at the sample coding standards in Example 5-3. They are intended to serve as a starting point for you and your team to begin the conversation about how CSS should be written in your project. Coding standards can be written and stored in any place that's convenient for you and your team, but they should be easily accessible so anybody can reference them.

Example 5-3. Example coding standards

1. Commenting:

    A. Each file should begin with a comment that explains what the file contains:

        ```
        /**
         * This file contains styles for tab groups.
         * Tab groups are intended to only contain elements with the tab class.
         */
        ```

    B. Properties that might be confusing should have a comment explaining them:

        ```
        .tab-group-flush {
            display: block;
            margin-left: -12px; /* removes parent container's padding */
            margin-right: -12px; /* removes parent container's padding */
        }
        ```

2. Formatting:

    A. Rulesets should:

        - appear on multiple lines when multiple properties are present
        - contain declarations that are indented 4 spaces

```
/* Incorrect */
.selector {
property1: value;
property2: value;
}

/* Incorrect */
.selector {
        property1: value;
        property2: value;
}

/* Incorrect */
.selector { property1: value; property2: value; }

/* Correct */
.selector {
    property1: value;
    property2: value;
}
```

B. Declarations should:

- contain one space after the colon
- always end with a semicolon

```
/* Incorrect */
.selector {
    property1:value;
}

/* Incorrect */
.selector {
    property1: value
}

/* Incorrect */
.selector {
    property1 : value;
}

/* Correct */
.selector {
    property1: value;
}
```

C. Rulesets may appear on one line only when multiple rulesets are
styling background-position differently

```
/* Incorrect */
.selector1 { property1: value; property2: value; }
.selector2 { property1: value; property2: value; }
```

```
.selector3 { property1: value; property2: value; }

/* Correct */
.selector1 { background-position: 0 0;     }
.selector2 { background-position: 0 -10px; }
.selector3 { background-position: 0 -10px; }
```

    D. Trailing whitespace must be removed from rulesets and declarations

2. Selector Naming Conventions:

    A. Only lowercase letters may be used

```
/* Incorrect */
.SeleCtor {}
.SELECTOR {}

/* Correct */
.selector {}
```

    B. Selectors with multiple words must use spinal-case

```
/* Incorrect: */
.selectorWithMultipleWords {}
.SELECTORWITHMULTIPLEWORDS {}
.selector_with_multiple_words {}
.selectorWith_multiple-words {}

/* Correct */
.selector-with-multiple-words {}
```

    C. IDs must not be used to style elements; use classes instead

```
/* Incorrect */
#element-to-style {}

/* Correct */
.element-to-style {}
```

    D. Style changes made by JavaScript (regardless of the framework used)
       must be done by adding or removing CSS classes

```
/**
 * Incorrect an element's style is changed via the style
 * attribute in JavaScript
 */
$('.js-menu-item').on('click', function (e) {
    $(this).css('background-color', '#FFFF00');
});

/**
 * Correct: an element's style is changed by adding a class with
```

```
 * JavaScript
 */
$('.js-menu-item').on('click', function (e) {
    $(this).addClass('highlighted');
});
```

E. Classes and IDs that are used as JavaScript selectors must be prefixed with js- and must not be present in a stylesheet

```
/**
 * Incorrect: styles prepended with js- should not be in a
 * stylesheet
 */
#js-element-only-used-by-javascript {
    background-color: #FFFF00;
}
```

```
/**
 * Incorrect: an element is selected in JavaScript by a class
 * used to style the element
 */
$('.menu-item').on('click', function () {
    $(this).addClass('highlighted');
});
```

```
/**
 * Correct: an element is selected in JavaScript by a selector
 * intended for JavaScript
 */
$('.js-menu-item').on('click', function () {
    $(this).addClass('highlighted');
});
```

F. Meaningful class names must be used

```
/* Incorrect: Class name is meaningless */
.r {}
```

```
/* Correct: Class name is meaningful and descriptive */
.resident {}
```

G. Class names must describe what is being styled as opposed to how it is being styled

```
/* Incorrect: describes style being applied */
.float-left-bold {}
```

```
/* Correct: describes what is being styled */
.sidebar-important {}
```

3. Properties

A. Shorthand properties may only be used for border, margin, and padding

```
/* Incorrect: shorthand is used for font property */
.selector {
    border: 1px solid #000000;
    font: 12px Arial, sans-serif;
}

/* Correct: shorthand is only used for border property */
.selector {
    border: 1px solid #000000;
    font-family: Arial, sans-serif;
    font-size: 12px;
}
```

B. Properties must be alphabetized

```
/* Incorrect */
.selector {
    padding: 12px;
    margin: 24px;
    border: 1px solid #000000;
}

/* Correct */
.selector {
    border: 1px solid #000000;
    margin: 24px;
    padding: 12px;
}
```

C. Properties with a value of 0 must omit the units

```
/* Incorrect */
.selector {
    padding: 0px;
    margin: 0px;
    border: 1px solid #000000;
}

/* Correct */
.selector {
    border: 1px solid #000000;
    margin: 0;
    padding: 0;
}
```

For more inspiration, take a look at these examples:

- Google CSS Coding Standards (*http://bit.ly/2e68N3y*)
- WordPress CSS Coding Standards (*http://bit.ly/2fgLrp2*)
- 18F Front End Guide (*https://pages.18f.gov/frontend/#css*)

Pattern Libraries

A *pattern library* (sometimes called a style guide) is a collection of user interface patterns that are used on a website and are displayed with information that is important relative to each pattern. Some of this information may include:

- Guidelines for when and when not to use a pattern
- Sample markup explaining how to use a pattern
- Information about why one pattern is used instead of a different one

Figure 5-20 is an example of a pattern library used by Yelp (*https://www.yelp.com/style guide*).

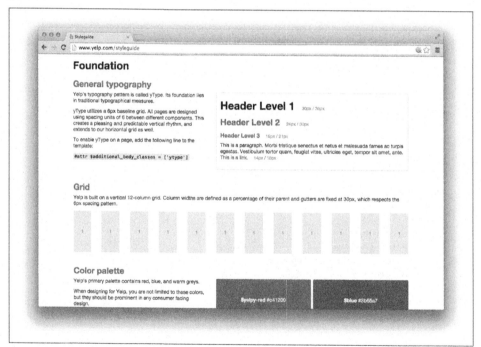

Figure 5-20. Yelp pattern library

Benefits

Pattern libraries are beneficial for a number of reasons. First, a pattern library provides a place where all of the components that make up a website can be seen. This gives everyone involved in a project the same access to the building blocks that make up the website and helps ensure that they are familiar with how things work. Familiarizing everyone with a reusable set of patterns will also provide the added benefit of making development faster because these building blocks won't need to be rebuilt from scratch for each new project.

Having everything in one place also encourages user interfaces to be built consistently. This can benefit a design team because it allows them to take inventory of existing patterns in the event that they need to change the way something looks. It also provides a constraint on design by encouraging new screens to be designed with these existing patterns, which further solidifies the idea that user interfaces should be consistent.

Finally, when all of the components that make up a website are displayed next to each other detecting inconsistencies becomes easier. Before deploying new code that affects the user interface, a pattern library provides a convenient place to look for visual regressions. When a change is made to a pattern and something doesn't look right, it becomes easier to diagnose the problem because the pattern is in its simplest form in a pattern library.

Building a pattern library

A pattern library doesn't need to be a work of art; it just needs to display each of the patterns and information about them. It can be as simple or complex as necessary. A pattern library should be available for everyone on the team to access in a public place so it can be consulted on a regular basis.

Building a pattern library should be a group effort because it encourages more people to familiarize themselves with the visual design patterns that are used on a website. Implementing a pattern library also provides a forum for team members to voice their opinions about everything from the user experience to its implementation, so a lot of new insight can come as a result of this effort. If you don't already have one, a pattern library should be first built to document the current condition of the user interface and then be iterated upon.

Pattern libraries promote the idea that styles have different intents and illustrate how styles should be combined like building blocks to build more complex patterns. Ideally each pattern should be documented with a working implementation of the pattern, notes about the pattern that include guidelines for when and when not to use it, and a code sample that shows how to implement the pattern. Pattern libraries also provide a terrific place to start visual regression testing. MailChimp's pattern library (*https://ux.mailchimp.com/patterns*) (Figure 5-21) does a great job of accomplishing all of these things.

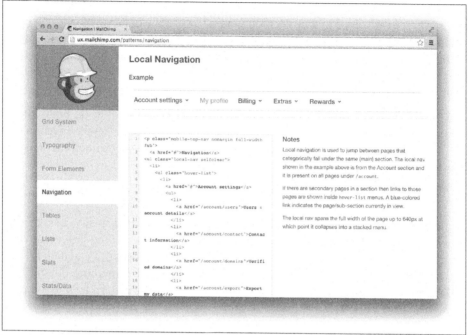

Figure 5-21. MailChimp's pattern library

More Resources

For more pattern library resources, including examples, articles, books, and podcasts, visit *http://styleguides.io*.

Chapter Summary

In this chapter we learned about testing CSS. We explored why testing CSS changes is time-consuming and difficult, thanks to the multiplicity of browsers and form factors that need to be tested. Resources were provided for obtaining new and old browsers, as well as emulators, virtual machines, and services for testing on other platforms. The benefits of establishing coding standards and pattern libraries were discussed, as well as visual regression testing with Gemini. With these tools at your disposal, testing CSS should be more approachable.

Code Placement and Refactoring Strategies

We've learned a lot about CSS: how the cascade works, the different intents styles can have, how to write better CSS, and how to effectively test it. This chapter first discusses how to organize your styles and then explores strategies for how to best refactor your CSS using everything we've learned. Then we'll wrap up by exploring how success can be measured after your code is refactored.

Organize CSS from Least Specific to Most Specific Styles

We learned in Chapter 2 that CSS styles are applied based on specificity and the order in which they are included. As such, it makes sense to organize your CSS in an order that is harmonious with how it will be applied:

1. Normalizing styles
2. Base styles
3. Styles for components and their containers
4. Structural styles
5. Utility styles
6. Browser-specific styles (if absolutely necessary)

This order includes CSS in such a way that as the declaration block selectors get more specific, more complicated selectors build off of the more general selectors that have already been included.

Here's a refresher on what the different types of styles are used for. As you read through the intents of these styles, notice how they build upon each other.

Normalizing Styles

We learned in Chapter 4 that normalizing styles are used for providing a starting point that irons out some of the inconsistencies between browsers. With these inconsistencies out of the way, styles that follow can benefit from the properties that have already been defined by these normalizing styles.

Base Styles

Base styles provide a starting point for all of the elements in the website. Things like spacing (`margin`, `padding`, `line-height`, etc.), font sizes and families, and anything else that can be used in the majority of styles that will not need to constantly be overridden should be included here.

Styles for Components and Their Containers

Component styles build on base styles and provide styling that makes use of visual metaphors to make it easier to interact with the website. As we learned, these styles should be written to work for the majority of use cases site-wide, and any changes in styling should be delegated to a parent container.

Structural Styles

Structural styles contain components and their containers. They are used to create the layout of a page and commonly define dimensions.

Utility Styles

Utility styles are among the most specific styles that should exist. Classes that get applied by JavaScript that make use of `!important` belong here, as do any other styles that serve a singular purpose.

Browser-Specific Styles

Finally, if you cannot drop support for legacy browsers, the styles you implement specifically for them belong here. These styles also likely make use of `!important` and are conditionally included in the website. They usually aren't very pretty, so be sure to delete them when they are no longer needed.

Keep Media Queries Close to Relevant Declaration Blocks

Media queries are used to style elements differently when certain conditions are met, like when a browser viewport is a particular width. Media queries should be kept close to the declaration blocks they style rather than placed at the end of the CSS or split them into a separate file. Doing so provides more context about how styles are applied.

Multiple Files or One Big File?

Code organization can be done in a couple of different ways, namely by using multiple files or one big file. It's important for developers to be able to work on their code easily with predictable code placement, but it's also really important that this be done in such a way that the website loads quickly for end users. First let's look at what happens when CSS is served to a browser, and then let's discuss developing with one file or multiple files.

Serving CSS

When someone visits a website that includes CSS files (as opposed to being styled by inline CSS) the browser requests those files, downloads them, and then parses them and applies the appropriate styles. Thus, it's important to make these downloads as small as possible so the site loads as quickly as possible.

Concatenation is the process of combining multiple files into one. It's a technique commonly used to decrease page load time by reducing the number of files that need to be downloaded. If the two files in Examples 6-1 and 6-2 were concatenated in that order, the result would be the file in Example 6-3.

Example 6-1. Example headings.css file

```
/**
 * This file contains styles for basic heading elements.
 */
h1 {
    color: #333;
    font-size: 24px;
    margin-bottom: 6px;
    margin-left: 12px;
    margin-right: 6px;
    margin-top: 12px;
}
```

Example 6-2. Example lists.css file

```
/**
 * This file contains styles for list elements.
 */
ul {
    list-style-type: none;
    padding-bottom: 12px;
    padding-left: 0;
    padding-top: 12px;
    padding-right: 0;
}
```

Example 6-3. Example concatenated CSS file

```
/**
 * This file contains styles for basic heading elements.
 */
h1 {
    color: #333;
    font-size: 24px;
    margin-bottom: 6px;
    margin-left: 12px;
    margin-right: 6px;
    margin-top: 12px;
}
/**
 * This file contains styles for list elements.
 */
ul {
    list-style-type: none;
    padding-bottom: 12px;
    padding-left: 0;
    padding-top: 12px;
    padding-right: 0;
}
```

Concatenation is powerful because it allows for big CSS files to be broken up into smaller files (which can then be reconstructed back into one big file, reducing page load time by reducing the number of files that the end user needs to download). Using multiple files allows for similar rulesets to be grouped together logically, so it becomes easier to find a particular piece of code. Additionally, using multiple files for development makes it easier to understand the contents of a CSS file without being overwhelmed, like you might be by one big file.

A concept that goes hand-in-hand with concatenating CSS files is minification. *Minification* is the process of removing all unneeded whitespace, comments, and newlines from files without changing their behavior. For example, when the code in

Example 6-1 and Example 6-2 is both concatenated and minified it will become the code in Example 6-4.

Example 6-4. Example CSS file after minification

```
h1{color:#333;font-size:24px;margin-bottom:6px;margin-left:12px;margin-right:6px;
margin-top:12px}ul{list-style-type:none;padding-bottom:12px;padding-left:0;
padding-top:12px;padding-right:0}
```

 Minified CSS usually appears on one line; the line breaks in this example are a result of formatting for this book.

Notice that all of the spaces and comments have been removed in Example 6-4. This is beneficial because spaces and comments increase the size of the CSS file that ultimately gets downloaded by the end user. By eliminating anything in the file that's unnecessary, the file can be made smaller. You should not try to write your code in a minified state, however, because doing so will lead to errors that are difficult to track down and it will be a nightmare to maintain.

There are any number of tools available online for concatenating and minifying CSS. When you're ready to take this step, research a couple of options and use whatever fits your needs. Maybe you just need to use one of the many simple websites that output minified CSS after being given unminified CSS, or maybe your needs are more complicated and you need something that augments your build process.

Developing with a Single File

For small projects, working in a single CSS file is perfectly acceptable and fairly easy. Based on the order in which CSS should be included such that it works with the cascade, the contents of this file can be organized into appropriately commented sections and subsections:

```
/**
 * Normalizing Styles
 * -------------------------------------------
 */

/**
 * Base Styles
 * -------------------------------------------
 */

/* Base Styles: Forms */
/* Base Styles: Headings */
/* Base Styles: Images */
```

```
/* Base Styles: Lists */
/* Base Styles: Tables */
/* etc. */

/**
 * Component Styles
 * --------------------------------------------
 */

/* Component Styles: Alerts */
/* Component Styles: Buttons */
/* Component Styles: Carousels */
/* Component Styles: Dropdowns */
/* Component Styles: Modals */
/* etc. */

/**
 * Structural Styles
 * --------------------------------------------
 */

/* Structural Styles: Checkout Layout */
/* Structural Styles: Sidebar Layout */
/* Structural Styles: Primary Layout */
/* Structural Styles: Settings Layout */
/* etc. */

/**
 * Utility Styles
 * --------------------------------------------
 */
```

Working in one CSS file can get difficult as the size of the project grows, though, and at some tipping point it will become evident that the CSS needs to be broken up into multiple files.

Developing with Multiple Files

When developing a website using multiple CSS files, file contents can be kept very focused. This can help prevent CSS from being added in a less optimal place if there is a correct file for it to be in. When developing with multiple CSS files your project might look something like this:

```
|-css/
|  |-normalizing-styles
|  |    |- normalize.css
|  |
|  |-base-styles
|  |    |- forms.css
|  |    |- headings.css
|  |    |- images.css
```

```
|   |   |- lists.css
|   |   |- tables.css
|   |   |- etc.
|   |
|   |-component-styles
|   |   |- alerts.css
|   |   |- buttons.css
|   |   |- carousel.css
|   |   |- dropdowns.css
|   |   |- modals.css
|   |   |- etc.
|   |
|   |- structural-styles
|   |   |- layout-checkout.css
|   |   |- layout-sidebar.css
|   |   |- layout-primary.css
|   |   |- layout-settings.css
|   |   |- etc.
|   |
|   |- utility-styles
|   |   |- utility.css
|   |
|   |- browser-specific-styles
|   |   |-ie8.css
```

With this many files, you shouldn't include each in your HTML as that many requests will slow down the page's load time. Development will be made much easier by an automated task that concatenates them into one file.

Auditing Your CSS Before Refactoring

It can be very helpful to get a high-level view of CSS metrics like:

- A list of properties being used
- A list of declaration blocks using a particular property
- The number of different colors being used
- The highest and lowest specificities that are used
- The selectors that have the highest and lowest specificities
- The length of selectors

CSS Dig is a free plug-in for the Google Chrome browser that can provide you with all of that information. To get it, visit *http://cssdig.com* using Chrome and install the plugin. Once you've installed it, you'll see the CSS Dig icon (Figure 6-1) next to the rest of the icons for browser extensions you've installed.

Figure 6-1. The CSS Dig extension icon

To use it, visit a website and click the CSS Dig icon. A modal window will appear that will present a list of CSS sources that can be analyzed as well as a list of files that cannot be analyzed (Figure 6-2).

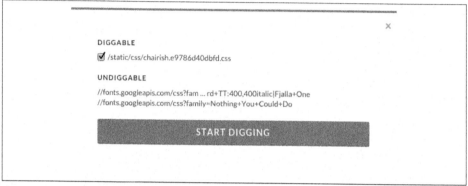

Figure 6-2. The CSS Dig modal prompt

Clicking through the prompt will instruct CSS Dig to analyze the available CSS, at which point it will present another modal that houses two tabs, Properties and Selectors, that provide information about both of those topics (Figure 6-3).

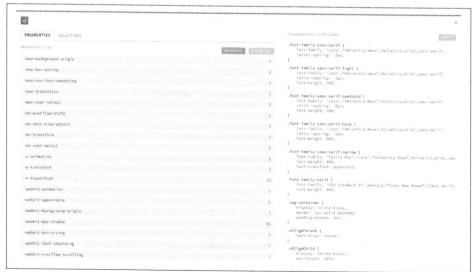

Figure 6-3. The CSS Dig Properties tab

As you'll see in the following sections, CSS Dig is an invaluable tool that will help you whip your code into shape.

Refactoring Strategies

This section explores strategies for how to approach refactoring your CSS. But first, a warning: when possible, refactoring should be done in small, manageable chunks that get reviewed and released frequently. If a lot of code is refactored and released at one time there is more risk for regression because more things have changed. Refactoring in large chunks can also delay writing code for new features and may require complicated merges in source control that can lead to regressions if not performed correctly. If code is refactored in small chunks there will be fewer changes that can cause regressions and the changes can be tested much more easily.

In Chapter 3 we learned a bunch of techniques for writing better CSS, but it can be overwhelming to implement them in a project that already has lots of code written. The end goal should be to employ all of these ideas, which will leave you with a CSS codebase that contains normalizing, base, component, container, structural, and utility styles. The following strategies should help you implement each idea, in an order that will encourage small changes that can be deployed sooner rather than later.

Consistently Structure Rulesets

Consistently structuring rulesets over time will make development much easier. Decide on how you want to format your declaration blocks and how declarations should be ordered. One way is to keep each declaration on its own line, in alphabetical order when possible. As you modify existing CSS or write new CSS, you can then make your rulesets more consistent with little risk.

Delete Dead Code

It's really important that you don't leave dead code in your CSS codebase. *Dead code* is code that is present but doesn't get used. In the context of CSS, it can take a couple of forms: unused declaration blocks, duplicate declaration blocks, and duplicate declarations.

Unused declaration blocks are declaration blocks that are present but never get used. Unused declaration blocks are a common occurrence because of human error; it can be difficult to keep track of which styles are used if code is written without a clear vision or lots of things have changed over time.

Duplicate declaration blocks are declaration blocks that are unnecessary because they are identical to other declaration blocks that already exist (Example 6-5). Duplicate declaration blocks usually come as a result of copying and pasting code.

Example 6-5. Duplicate declaration blocks

```
h1 {
    font-size: 28px;
    font-weight: 900;
}

/* This is a duplicate declaration block */
h1 {
    font-size: 28px;
    font-weight: 900;
}
```

Similarly, *duplicate declarations* (Example 6-6) are declarations that are identical to other declarations in the same declaration block. It's common to have duplicate declarations in different rulesets, and this is fine because the cascade will sort things out for us (though these styles should be combined when possible). However, duplicate declarations in the same ruleset should be avoided because the last occurring declaration will be applied, rendering the ones before it useless.

Example 6-6. Duplicate declaration blocks

```
h1 {
    font-size: 28px;
    font-weight: 900;
    font-weight: 900; /* This is a duplicate declaration */
}

.section-title {
    font-size: 24px;
    /* This is not a duplicate declaration because it appears
     * in a different declaration block for a different selector
     */
    font-weight: 900;
}
```

Dead code is bad because it makes your codebase more confusing than it needs to be, which makes it more difficult to maintain. When you go to change code you're probably pretty careful to make sure it doesn't break anything, and this can take up a lot of your time if there are large amounts of dead CSS to wade through. On top of that, CSS gets sent from your server to the end user's browser, so when you have lots of dead code your CSS files take longer to download, which detracts from a good user experience (especially on a slow connection).

Decouple CSS and JavaScript

Classes and IDs that are used to style elements shouldn't be used to select them in JavaScript because it creates a dependency that makes changing those selectors difficult. Early on, CSS and JavaScript should be decoupled because it's likely that classes and IDs will be changed and that could result in broken JavaScript.

Decoupling CSS and JavaScript is as easy as searching your JavaScript for places where elements are selected, then prepending the selector with `js-` and adding that selector to the HTML where the element is defined.

If you're using a JavaScript framework, consult the framework's documentation for how to select elements and then search for places where that's done in your JavaScript. If your code doesn't make use of a framework, searching for the string `document.getElement` should reveal where elements are being selected by either `document.getElementById` or `document.getElementsByClassName`, which should be a good starting point. Finding the HTML that contains the element being selected is as easy as searching for the original class or ID that was used in the JavaScript.

Separate Base Styles

Base styles should be the simplest styles in any website because they make use of type selectors. After analyzing a website with CSS Dig, the Selectors panel (Figure 6-4) provides a tremendous amount of insight as to when and where a selector is used.

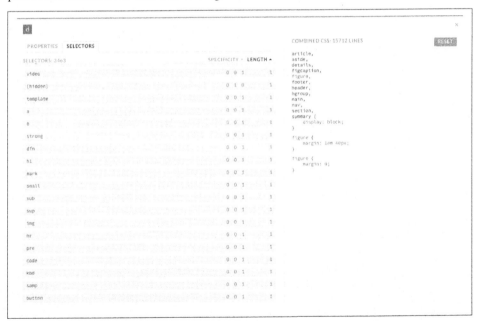

Figure 6-4. The CSS Dig Selectors panel

Make a list of your base styles as different groups:

- Headings (<h1>–<h6>)
- Text (e.g., <p>, <fig>, <code>)
- Links (<a>)
- Lists (<dl>, <ol>, <ul>)
- Forms (e.g., <form>, <legend>, <fieldset>, <input>, <button>)
- Tables (e.g., <table>, <thead>, <tbody>, <tfoot>, <tr>, <td>)
- Media (e.g., <audio>, <object>, <video>)

Once this is done you can use CSS Dig to look for selectors that fall into a particular category. After identifying how often and where the selectors are used, you can compare them and see which properties are common. If a type selector is only used alone and appears once, then it can be safely moved. However, if a type selector is used multiple times, these are the steps to follow:

1. Create a new ruleset in your base styles for the type selector whose styles are being refactored.

2. Copy the most common properties found among all uses of the type selector into the new ruleset.

3. Remove duplicative properties from other rulesets that can be inherited from the new base style.

For example, let's assume that CSS Dig found there were multiple styles defined for the <h1> tag, as shown in Example 6-7.

Example 6-7. Multiple styles For <h1>

```
/* File: styles.css */

h1 {
    color: #000000;
    font-family: Helvetica, sans-serif;
    font-size: 32px;
    line-height: 1.2;
}

body > div > h1 {
    color: #000000;
    font-size: 32px;
    margin-bottom: 12px;
}
```

```css
.section-condensed h1 {
    color: #000000;
    font-size: 16px;
}

.order-form h1 {
    font-family: Helvetica, sans-serif;
    color: #333333;
    text-decoration: underline;
}
```

The first step is to create a new ruleset:

```css
/* File: headings.css */

h1 {

}
```

Next, copy the most common styles into the new ruleset:

```css
/* File: headings.css */

h1 {
    color: #000000;
    font-family: Helvetica, sans-serif;
    font-size: 32px;
    line-height: 1.2;
}
```

Finally, remove duplicate styles from rulesets that can instead inherit them from base styles:

```css
/* File: styles.css */

body > div > h1 {
    margin-bottom: 12px;
}

.section-condensed h1 {
    font-size: 16px;
}

.order-form h1 {
    color: #333333;
    text-decoration: underline;
}
```

If something doesn't look right after making these changes, inspect the element with your favorite browser's developer tools and check the CSS panel to determine where the problematic styles are coming from. If the problem cannot be rectified easily, then temporary styles with a more specific selector can be written to overcome the issue. Be sure to leave behind a comment indicating that the styles are temporary and why they are necessary. As you continue to refactor, you'll eventually be able to remove these temporary styles.

Finally, the styles that are *not* included in the base styles can be scrutinized to see if they are deviating from what the styles are intended to be. If this is the case, then the styles that deviate can be removed.

Remove Redundant IDs

In CSS files, selectors with the highest specificities will make use of IDs. Selectors that have multiple IDs in them can be refactored first by eliminating everything to the left of the rightmost ID. Because IDs can be used at most once on any given page, having multiple IDs in a selector is redundant. For example, the selector in Example 6-9 will select the same element styled in Example 6-8, but it will have a lower specificity. If lowering the specificity of one element cannot be done because it is overriding styles from an even more specific selector, the more specific selector should have its specificity reduced first.

Example 6-8. Redundant IDs in a selector

```
#main-header > div > div > ul#main-menu {
    border-bottom: 1px solid #000000;
}
```

Example 6-9. Redundant IDs removed from a selector

```
#main-menu {
    border-bottom: 1px solid #000000;
}
```

Convert IDs to Classes

Once redundant IDs are removed, the remaining selectors that make use of IDs can be converted to use classes instead. This process will take some time, but in the end you'll be left with CSS that has a much lower specificity that can be reused much more easily when needed. When changing IDs to classes remember to use meaningful names rather than cryptic or overly specific names.

When you switch to using classes, you may find that some elements are no longer styled as intended because of the decreased specificity. This can potentially be fixed by decreasing the specificity of the selectors whose styles are overriding the styles with lower specificity. However, if changes to lots of other selectors are required to fix a particular problem, then you're probably better off not changing the ID to a class and instead waiting to refactor this piece of code until the more specific styles have themselves been refactored to have a lower specificity.

Separate Utility Styles

Utility styles are the only styles that should be making use of the `!important` exception. Searching your CSS for `!important` should hopefully turn up few results, but those that do appear and have a single purpose (hiding an element, for example) should be grouped together as utility styles. Earlier in this chapter we determined that utility styles should appear at the bottom when your CSS is concatenated, so be sure to order these styles properly when combining your files.

Styles that are not utility styles that make use of the `!important` exception should be analyzed using your favorite browser's developer tools to determine why it is being used. If it turns out `!important` doesn't need to be used, then it can safely be removed. However, if `!important` is being used to override inherited styles, then leave it alone for the time being and leave behind a comment explaining why it is being used. When the styles `!important` is overriding are refactored, this piece of code can be revisited and refactored, and it can safely be removed.

Define Reusable Components

Defining reusable components can be one of the most daunting tasks when refactoring CSS because there is usually a fear of not getting it right the first time. This fear is unfounded, though, because even if you don't get things 100% right the first time, you can always revisit them in the future and make them right.

Start off by choosing one interface pattern that gets reused frequently (e.g., tabs) and spending some time surveying your website and noting the places where that pattern is used. Make note of any variations of the pattern and decide whether those variations are legitimate or came into existence as a result of inconsistent CSS. Follow the guidelines for building reusable components in "Component Styles" on page 54, and then update all of the occurrences of the pattern to use that code.

Defining reusable components aids in eliminating duplicate CSS and, usually, the remaining IDs that are used to style elements as well. When an interface pattern that could be a reusable component is written for the first time everything is great, but when a similar but slightly different pattern is defined, much of the CSS from the first occurrence is copied and tweaked to meet the needs of the newer, slightly different interface pattern. This duplication can be prevented by making use of the same component styles, but redefining them by delegating that responsibility to either a container group or structural styles.

Remove Inline CSS and Over-Modularized Classes

Removing inline CSS and over-modularized classes should be done at the same time because they're essentially the same thing, though inline CSS that appears in the `style` attribute has a much higher specificity unless it is overridden using the `!important` exception. In both cases, this should be done later rather than sooner.

If you've been refactoring in the order presented in this chapter, then by now you:

- Are on your way to having your CSS structured consistently
- Have less dead code
- Have decoupled your CSS from your JavaScript
- Have established base styles
- Have lowered your highest specificities by removing redundant IDs and converting IDs to classes
- Have separated out utility styles and reduced the use of `!important`
- Have defined reusable components

After all of that, you now have a place to migrate inline styles to—if you have any left! Had you removed inline CSS earlier on, you would have needed to temporarily place it in interim classes at the end of your stylesheets and possibly use `!important` to ensure it maintained specificity. If you wait, though, all you have to do is search your HTML for inline styles and either remove them if they are no longer needed or move them into the appropriate places in your stylesheets. Again, inline styles that deviate from base and component styles should be investigated to determine if this was a result of inconsistent design or coding. If this is the case, then the inline styles can safely be removed. If the variation is intentional, then the styles should likely be used to modify an element via its container.

Segregate Browser-Specific CSS Hacks

Not all browsers are created equal, and as a result it's easy to pollute CSS with hacks to get around browser limitations. But before you segregate browser-specific hacks, remember to look at your website's traffic and determine if you can drop support for that browser instead. Deleting browser hacks is much easier and more satisfying than refactoring this code into its own home. In the event that you cannot drop support for a browser, all you need to do is style an element specifically for that browser using the conditional comment technique from Chapter 4.

Measuring Success

After everything we've learned, it's important to understand how success can be determined so there are achievable goals to strive for when refactoring. Following are a number of ideas for how success can be measured after refactoring CSS. Some of the recommendations here, like inspecting file sizes, should also be done before refactoring so they can be compared with the results after.

Is Your Website Broken?

The first and most obvious way to determine success after refactoring code is to find out if its behavior has changed in a negative way. Remember, refactoring is the process of rewriting code to make it simpler *without* changing its behavior. In Chapter 5 we discussed using multiple browsers to test by hand as well as testing visual regressions through taking screenshots. If no visual regressions are detected after thorough visual inspection, then it's time to consider some of the other aspects.

Low coupling

Quality CSS is decoupled from the structure of the HTML it is used in. You can decouple your CSS from your HTML by creating reusable components and containing elements, using the strategies found in Chapter 4. While there is always going to be some degree of coupling, avoiding overly complex selectors is a reasonable goal to strive for. Tools like CSS Dig can help you sniff out complex and overqualified selectors that should be made more general. Audit your site and inspect your selectors to see where improvements are necessary.

Low specificities

We learned in Chapter 2 that CSS specificity and ruleset order are used to determine which styles are applied to an element. We also learned strategies in Chapter 4 that can and should be used to decrease overall CSS specificity. Selector specificity is a metric that can be measured and used to determine if a CSS codebase contains an abundance of selectors with high specificities that will be difficult to maintain. Tools like CSS Dig can sort selectors by this characteristic.

Fewer files and smaller file sizes

We learned earlier in this chapter that concatenation and minification should be used when serving CSS files to end users—concatenation reduces the number of files that need to be downloaded, and minification reduces the file size by removing unnecessary characters. Both of these processes result in faster downloads, which in turn results in faster page load times. To measure this metric you can simply compare the sum of all CSS file sizes before refactoring with the sum of all CSS file sizes after refactoring.

Number of UI Bugs

Once you begin refactoring your CSS and making use of coding standards, the number of UI bugs as a result of messy or duplicative code should decrease. As we learned in Chapter 5, implementing a UI pattern library and monitoring visual regressions using screenshots are great ways to ensure the user interface is built using code that has been tested thoroughly and is monitored for regressions over time. Software bugs are inevitable—they can be introduced by website developers, or browser issues can be introduced by browser makers—but using a pattern library and visual regression testing are surefire ways that you'll be able to detect and diagnose these issues faster than you might be able to otherwise.

Reduced Development and Testing Time

After logically organizing your CSS into multiple files, establishing coding standards, and creating a UI pattern library you will hopefully be able to build and maintain user interfaces faster than ever. This metric is highly individual, because some interfaces are much more complicated than others, which means they will take more time to build. For the most part, though, you'll probably be able to tell if your development time has decreased as a result of refactoring and enhancing your workflow.

In addition to reducing the time spent in development, you might also notice that you're able to test your interfaces much faster than before if you have the right tools at your disposal. Again, all of the methods for testing that we discussed in Chapter 5 should help you test your interfaces more quickly with a higher level of confidence.

Chapter Summary

In this chapter we discussed how CSS should be organized, strategies for refactoring your code, and how to measure success. Remember that when using these strategies it's important to use them over time rather than all at once, so changes can be released in smaller, more controlled chunks. When you begin implementing the strategies described in this chapter you'll be on your way to building a CSS codebase that adheres to all of the tenets of good architecture.

normalize.css

```
/*! normalize.css v5.0.0 | MIT License | github.com/necolas/normalize.css */

/**
 * 1. Change the default font family in all browsers (opinionated).
 * 2. Correct the line height in all browsers.
 * 3. Prevent adjustments of font size after orientation changes in
 *    IE on Windows Phone and in iOS.
 */

/* Document
   ========================================================================== */

html {
  font-family: sans-serif; /* 1 */
  line-height: 1.15; /* 2 */
  -ms-text-size-adjust: 100%; /* 3 */
  -webkit-text-size-adjust: 100%; /* 3 */
}

/* Sections
   ========================================================================== */

/**
 * Remove the margin in all browsers (opinionated).
 */

body {
  margin: 0;
}

/**
 * Add the correct display in IE 9-.
 */
```

```
article,
aside,
footer,
header,
nav,
section {
  display: block;
}

/**
 * Correct the font size and margin on `h1` elements within `section` and
 * `article` contexts in Chrome, Firefox, and Safari.
 */

h1 {
  font-size: 2em;
  margin: 0.67em 0;
}

/* Grouping content
   ================================================================== */

/**
 * Add the correct display in IE 9-.
 * 1. Add the correct display in IE.
 */

figcaption,
figure,
main { /* 1 */
  display: block;
}

/**
 * Add the correct margin in IE 8.
 */

figure {
  margin: 1em 40px;
}

/**
 * 1. Add the correct box sizing in Firefox.
 * 2. Show the overflow in Edge and IE.
 */

hr {
  box-sizing: content-box; /* 1 */
  height: 0; /* 1 */
  overflow: visible; /* 2 */
}
```

```
/**
 * 1. Correct the inheritance and scaling of font size in all browsers.
 * 2. Correct the odd `em` font sizing in all browsers.
 */

pre {
  font-family: monospace, monospace; /* 1 */
  font-size: 1em; /* 2 */
}

/* Text-level semantics
   ================================================================ */

/**
 * 1. Remove the gray background on active links in IE 10.
 * 2. Remove gaps in links underline in iOS 8+ and Safari 8+.
 */

a {
  background-color: transparent; /* 1 */
  -webkit-text-decoration-skip: objects; /* 2 */
}

/**
 * Remove the outline on focused links when they are also active or hovered
 * in all browsers (opinionated).
 */

a:active,
a:hover {
  outline-width: 0;
}

/**
 * 1. Remove the bottom border in Firefox 39-.
 * 2. Add the correct text decoration in Chrome, Edge, IE, Opera, and Safari.
 */

abbr[title] {
  border-bottom: none; /* 1 */
  text-decoration: underline; /* 2 */
  text-decoration: underline dotted; /* 2 */
}

/**
 * Prevent the duplicate application of `bolder` by the next rule in Safari 6.
 */

b,
strong {
  font-weight: inherit;
}
```

```
/**
 * Add the correct font weight in Chrome, Edge, and Safari.
 */

b,
strong {
  font-weight: bolder;
}

/**
 * 1. Correct the inheritance and scaling of font size in all browsers.
 * 2. Correct the odd `em` font sizing in all browsers.
 */

code,
kbd,
samp {
  font-family: monospace, monospace; /* 1 */
  font-size: 1em; /* 2 */
}

/**
 * Add the correct font style in Android 4.3-.
 */

dfn {
  font-style: italic;
}

/**
 * Add the correct background and color in IE 9-.
 */

mark {
  background-color: #ff0;
  color: #000;
}

/**
 * Add the correct font size in all browsers.
 */

small {
  font-size: 80%;
}

/**
 * Prevent `sub` and `sup` elements from affecting the line height in
 * all browsers.
 */
```

```css
sub,
sup {
  font-size: 75%;
  line-height: 0;
  position: relative;
  vertical-align: baseline;
}

sub {
  bottom: -0.25em;
}

sup {
  top: -0.5em;
}

/* Embedded content
   ================================================================= */

/**
 * Add the correct display in IE 9-.
 */

audio,
video {
  display: inline-block;
}

/**
 * Add the correct display in iOS 4-7.
 */

audio:not([controls]) {
  display: none;
  height: 0;
}

/**
 * Remove the border on images inside links in IE 10-.
 */

img {
  border-style: none;
}

/**
 * Hide the overflow in IE.
 */

svg:not(:root) {
  overflow: hidden;
}
```

```
/* Forms
   ================================================================ */

/**
 * 1. Change the font styles in all browsers (opinionated).
 * 2. Remove the margin in Firefox and Safari.
 */

button,
input,
optgroup,
select,
textarea {
  font-family: sans-serif; /* 1 */
  font-size: 100%; /* 1 */
  line-height: 1.15; /* 1 */
  margin: 0; /* 2 */
}

/**
 * Show the overflow in IE.
 * 1. Show the overflow in Edge.
 */

button,
input { /* 1 */
  overflow: visible;
}

/**
 * Remove the inheritance of text transform in Edge, Firefox, and IE.
 * 1. Remove the inheritance of text transform in Firefox.
 */

button,
select { /* 1 */
  text-transform: none;
}

/**
 * 1. Prevent a WebKit bug where (2) destroys native `audio` and `video`
 *    controls in Android 4.
 * 2. Correct the inability to style clickable types in iOS and Safari.
 */

button,
html [type="button"], /* 1 */
[type="reset"],
[type="submit"] {
  -webkit-appearance: button; /* 2 */
}
```

```
/**
 * Remove the inner border and padding in Firefox.
 */

button::-moz-focus-inner,
[type="button"]::-moz-focus-inner,
[type="reset"]::-moz-focus-inner,
[type="submit"]::-moz-focus-inner {
  border-style: none;
  padding: 0;
}

/**
 * Restore the focus styles unset by the previous rule.
 */

button:-moz-focusring,
[type="button"]:-moz-focusring,
[type="reset"]:-moz-focusring,
[type="submit"]:-moz-focusring {
  outline: 1px dotted ButtonText;
}

/**
 * Change the border, margin, and padding in all browsers (opinionated).
 */

fieldset {
  border: 1px solid #c0c0c0;
  margin: 0 2px;
  padding: 0.35em 0.625em 0.75em;
}

/**
 * 1. Correct the text wrapping in Edge and IE.
 * 2. Correct the color inheritance from `fieldset` elements in IE.
 * 3. Remove the padding so developers are not caught out when they zero out
 *    `fieldset` elements in all browsers.
 */

legend {
  box-sizing: border-box; /* 1 */
  color: inherit; /* 2 */
  display: table; /* 1 */
  max-width: 100%; /* 1 */
  padding: 0; /* 3 */
  white-space: normal; /* 1 */
}

/**
 * 1. Add the correct display in IE 9-.
```

```
 * 2. Add the correct vertical alignment in Chrome, Firefox, and Opera.
 */

progress {
  display: inline-block; /* 1 */
  vertical-align: baseline; /* 2 */
}

/**
 * Remove the default vertical scrollbar in IE.
 */

textarea {
  overflow: auto;
}

/**
 * 1. Add the correct box sizing in IE 10-.
 * 2. Remove the padding in IE 10-.
 */

[type="checkbox"],
[type="radio"] {
  box-sizing: border-box; /* 1 */
  padding: 0; /* 2 */
}

/**
 * Correct the cursor style of increment and decrement buttons in Chrome.
 */

[type="number"]::-webkit-inner-spin-button,
[type="number"]::-webkit-outer-spin-button {
  height: auto;
}

/**
 * 1. Correct the odd appearance in Chrome and Safari.
 * 2. Correct the outline style in Safari.
 */

[type="search"] {
  -webkit-appearance: textfield; /* 1 */
  outline-offset: -2px; /* 2 */
}

/**
 * Remove the inner padding and cancel buttons in Chrome and Safari on macOS.
 */

[type="search"]::-webkit-search-cancel-button,
[type="search"]::-webkit-search-decoration {
```

```
  -webkit-appearance: none;
}

/**
 * 1. Correct the inability to style clickable types in iOS and Safari.
 * 2. Change font properties to `inherit` in Safari.
 */

::-webkit-file-upload-button {
  -webkit-appearance: button; /* 1 */
  font: inherit; /* 2 */
}

/* Interactive
   ============================================================ */

/*
 * Add the correct display in IE 9-.
 * 1. Add the correct display in Edge, IE, and Firefox.
 */

details, /* 1 */
menu {
  display: block;
}

/*
 * Add the correct display in all browsers.
 */

summary {
  display: list-item;
}

/* Scripting
   ============================================================ */

/**
 * Add the correct display in IE 9-.
 */

canvas {
  display: inline-block;
}

/**
 * Add the correct display in IE.
 */

template {
  display: none;
}
```

```
/* Hidden
   ============================================================ */

/**
 * Add the correct display in IE 10-.
 */

[hidden] {
  display: none;
}
```

Index

L

:link pseudoclass, 47
links, base style for, 48
lists, base style for, 49
Litmus (testing service), 86

M

MailChimp, pattern library, 106
maintainability, 2
margin property, inheritance and, 43
media queries, keeping close to relevant declaration block, 109
metadata, document, 44
Microsoft Edge/Internet Explorer
    developer tools, 86
        emulating device sizes, 90
    DOM and CSS styles, 92
    download site, 79
    downloading old versions for testing, 84
    early releases for Microsoft Edge, 85
    most-used versions, 76
    ms vendor prefix, 29
minification, 110
mobile browsers, 79
moz vendor prefix, 29
Mozilla Firefox (see Firefox)
ms vendor prefix, 29

N

normalize.css, 42
normalizing styles, 42, 108

O

ordered and unordered lists, base style for, 49
over-modularization
    avoiding over-modularized classes, 37
    removing over-modularized classes, 122
overqualified selectors, 31

P

padding property, inheritance and, 43
Parallels, 84
pattern libraries, 104
    benefits of, 105
    building, 105
performant selectors, 32
PhantomCSS, 98
PhantomJS, 94

predictability of good architectures, 2
properties, x
    defined, xi
    inherited values in CSS, 44
    organizing with vendor prefixes in rulesets, 29
    setting for base styles, 43
pseudoclasses, 47

Q

qualified selectors, appropriate use of, 31

R

refactoring
    defined, 1
    examples, 5-20
        calculating total for ecommerce order, 6
        displaying the headline of a website, 17
    factors leading to, 3
    measuring success of, 122-124
    permissions for, 5
    software architecture and, 2
    strategies for, 115-122
        consistently structuring rulesets, 115
        converting IDs to classes, 120
        decoupling CSS and JavaScript, 117
        defining reusable components, 121
        deleting dead code, 115
        removing inline CSS and over-modularized classes, 122
        removing redundant IDs, 120
        segregating browser-specific CSS hacks, 122
        separating base styles, 117
        separating utility styles, 121
    when not to do it, 4
    when to do it, 4
requirements, changes in, 3
reusable components, 54
    defining, 121
ruleset order, 23
rulesets, xi
    duplicate declarations in, 116
    structuring consistently, 28, 115

S

Safari browsers, 84
    developer tools, 86